Underground

Underground

New and Selected Poems

JIM MOORE

Graywolf Press

The New Body was originally published by the University of Pittsburgh Press in 1975. *The Freedom of History* was originally published by Milkweed Editions in 1988. *The Long Experience of Love* was originally published by Milkweed Editions in 1995. *Writing with Tagore: Homages and Variations* was originally published by the Press at Colorado College in 2003. *Lightning at Dinner* was originally published by Graywolf Press in 2005. *Invisible Strings* was originally published by Graywolf Press in 2011.

This publication is made possible, in part, by the voters of Minnesota through a Minnesota State Arts Board Operating Support grant, thanks to a legislative appropriation from the arts and cultural heritage fund, and through grants from the National Endowment for the Arts and the Wells Fargo Foundation Minnesota. Significant support has also been provided by Target, the McKnight Foundation, Amazon.com, and other generous contributions from foundations, corporations, and individuals. To these organizations and individuals we offer our heartfelt thanks.

Published by Graywolf Press
250 Third Avenue North, Suite 600
Minneapolis, Minnesota 55401

www.graywolfpress.org

Published in the United States of America

ISBN 978-1-55597-687-3

2 4 6 8 9 7 5 3 1
First Graywolf Printing, 2014

Library of Congress Control Number: 2014935700

Cover design: Kyle G. Hunter

Cover photo: JoAnn Verburg, *Underground,* © 2005.

This book is for my family:

for JoAnn,
for Madeline and Mira, for Bonnie and Robbie, for Carol

CONTENTS

from *Writing with Tagore: Homages and Variations* (2003)

from *Lightning at Dinner* (2005)

from *Invisible Strings* (2011)

Twenty Questions: New Poems (2014)

Underground

from

THE NEW BODY

(1975)

TWO FLUTE SONGS

1

I want to become thin as a flute song
which goes into the delicate inner ear
and coils there, holding in balance the lives
of everyone I love.

2

It's late and the furnace goes full blast
filling the room like a good joke.
I read aloud, pausing for rain.
If my pipe were alive
I could not hold it more lovingly.
Soon, I will make green tea
and pray that the flute song I barely hear
is not a signal for dawn
and is not a record, nor an answer
to any questions I might pose it.

WOLF

1

The wolf always comes at the last moment,
alone. He is never full,
you never can throw him enough bones.
When I see a wolf, even a photograph,
I shiver.
Something taut and frozen inside me wants to stretch on and on;
winter river, glint after glint stretched out under the sun.

2

This is the wolf:
what is left when you've tried to throw everything away.
Part of him lives in the city
where people stand in record stores at midnight
and move through the stacks,
their hands stumbling, confused,
abandoned, expected to make their way . . .

3

To find the wolf
look at anything wary, anything falling down.
That old woman on West Seventh
directing traffic with a torn branch,
the tree all twisted from growing between apartment houses.
Or the time I lifted the garbage can lid
finding the flowers
from when the baby downstairs died,
turned on their side in the bottom of the can;
bright yellow, still growing in the darkness.

AT THE LAUNDROMAT

I sat at the very end of the laundromat,
so old there wasn't even Muzak, no shiny pink washing machines,
the ceiling full of peeling paint like a book with its pages burned.
My eyes felt thick, my sight poured out of me in columns, focused,
I *saw*, say "saw" slowly three times and you will feel the odd heft of this
    vision:
saw, saw, saw,
the way I felt my third night out of prison when we walked through a
    stubble field
to the river I had never seen by daylight and sat there
in the cool October night, the river below us down a steep bank,
sat there watching the blackness for many minutes,
felt the black motion of my own heavy body for the first time in ten
    months
and in that laundromat the blackness came again, everything there
heavy with use, the huge ceiling fan encrusted with dirt, each blade
    thick with it
and at the other end the short man in the green shirt who ran the place,
one of those puke green knit shirts buttoned to the top,
he sorted laundry, slowly, very slowly, taking each piece out of the dryers,
shaking it once, holding it to the light, shaking it again,
then (if it were coat or shirt) lifting it to his nose
and smelling the armpits, smelling each one carefully
and finally hanging them in a long row ready for pickup.

It was late, almost 10 P.M., and he called out to another laundromat.
At first he seemed happy, then angry as he complained bitterly,
how they hadn't cleaned the machines,
how he would shake them up good soon, how they listened to the
    radio—
no more radios!—it was quarter to ten and they still had time to do the
    windows.

My whole body then was with his body, I felt the rising anger in us both,
heavy, weighted, each in our clumsy bodies. I could feel
the pull of him, as if dragging me across the dance floor,
teaching me a new step, no
future, no future, our hands sunk to the elbows in soap,
twisting shirts into rags, sinking the rags one by one,
cleaning the dry grains of soap off the table tops for the last time,
removing the thumb prints from the plate glass,
pulling back the tab on the cash register, making the room black.

THE HISTORY OF ROSES

7 A.M. first frost, the nurse who works all night
walks home, feet splayed gingerly in two directions.
Last night the old man who sells papers by day and flowers by night
sold us roses, five for a dollar. And the world
sways a little on its stem at how people have to shuffle to survive.

And now there are roses on your desk, concentrated slices of dawn,
darkened, folded into layers, veined and bunched together,
coil of soft petals above the delicate green leaves.
And the history of roses is the history of the work whistle,
the florist for whom the holidays are a nightmare,
whose children are asleep by the time he's home Christmas Eve,
who stands alone in the kitchen he remodeled and eats a dish of ice cream
before he goes to bed: he is still young when his first heart attack comes.

There is no end to the history of roses, to blooming and quiet,
to what withers and returns. All knowledge hurts:
and when we walk out of a theater and buy roses
there have to be tears and oceans and blind trust
in the clot of a dark red substance on the end of a cut stem.

RESOLUTIONS

This year I'll be a hair shirt in reverse,
teeth on fruit and a tongue in the secret places,
a psalm in the face of my enemies,
the nail that works loose from every theory,
two steps toward whatever moves,
a cool basement for my goat to play in,
and this year I'll take ten fingers
and write slowly of the prisons,
no sadness will be spared,
no cell forgotten,
and every day I'll remember
the length of each convict's body.
I'll remember the new year is everywhere,
even behind those bars,
and join my friends in the tunnels
where in spite of everything
Terry danced a jig once and I watched
and I think I'll bathe in the sea
and let no more than a little salt water
separate Terry and me.

COMING BACK FOR HELP

for Tom McGrath

We have all the poems about darkness and hidden water,
sad attempts to take us away from ourselves,
to find the boats
without captains that will return us to the sea,
will float us into perfection,
perfect sailors of the unconscious.
Is solitude so bleak?
Do we become perfect as we strip our lives of affection,
is snow blindness the final absolution?

It is winter now in Saint Paul. I am alone,
I love my teacup with its bird under the curved flower,
the way sunlight illuminates the little clouds of dust-hair in my room
and in the evening the sound of a radio floats in from down the street,
the voice of the announcer sad in its forced intensity.

Voice,
they would give you a funeral at sea,
but you'll come back,
message scribbled in a bottle
crying for help
because we always do,
no matter how we long
to finger
the stone harp of purity
in the coldest water
of the most inhuman ocean.

MUSIC

for Meridel LeSueur

1

The cold egg of the snow cracks open,
broadens into chunks of fog.
10 A.M. and the street corner is invisible.
I turn on the electric heater, listen to Casals,
watch the branches like thin asparagus stalks
shrouded and growing under water.
Something lives here bigger than my skin,
larger even than the old man Pablo bent over his bow,
the old man Pablo brushing his quick strokes on paper,
the old man Pablo writing his last poem from a hospital bed.

At the trial they are talking about death.
The old Indians have faces that crease in all directions,
crisscrossed patches of flesh, long black hair.
Hundreds are indicted.
The young prosecutor wears a sweater under his jacket to keep off the cold.
And the deaths at Wounded Knee hover somewhere in that dark fog.
Nothing is lost,
nothing disappears. The murders dissolve and then re-form into
    something new.

2

Night now.
Quarter moon behind trees.
Down the block the yellow-lemon light is always there.
At sunset the last of the fog was caught, pink, like a glaze separated from
    its pot.
Today in Spain two anarchists from the mountains garroted:
a leather collar with a nail sticking out is placed around the neck and
    tightened.
The moon clears the trees now and hangs free in the sky, bodiless.

3

Three days ago I bought a Zuni bracelet, thought about it
a long time, wore it around the shop and shook my wrist like a dancer
trying on new shoes. There are small pieces of turquoise and coral,
bits of the mastodon world like a speck caught in the eye.
Vision of the small, tears from another culture set in silver.
The silver in the bracelet shivers in sunlight, glows in candlelight;
a white arc of music for the eye,
vibrations scattered like small campfires along a beach.
I see cello
phosphorescence, curved fingers along the bow,
an old man's notations thrown back over his shoulder.

AT 7 A.M., WATCHING THE CARS ON THE BRIDGE

Everybody's going to work. Well,
not me. I'm not
going to work.

HOW TO CLOSE THE GREAT DISTANCE
BETWEEN PEOPLE

Do it over coffee,
like fish that appear to be talking,
but are really eating to stay alive.

SUNSET

1

The sun spins off into its last corner
down by the steel webbing that supports water towers,
down every stalk, into the stones with their layers of blackness,
giving breath to dust and blood to loneliness.

A kite string breaks,
the kite floats like a detached wing, single wing-tip
through the narrowing band of light, high
over Applebaum's neon sign,
away into the valley, over the curve of the small houses in the Czech
    neighborhood.

All falls down.
Light glitters along the frozen edges of the turnpike.
Chromatic dismembering,
totally alone in the changing scales of light
like a small boy standing in the dusk of his parents' bedroom.
Downstairs the babysitter watches TV. The boy stands by his father's
    bureau
and sees the familiar neighborhood go dark, sees the trees
on Reising's hill, their branches like huge nests in the last light.

Children in the dusk.
The last line of carelessness,
jump ropes cutting a floating erratic arc in the purple sky.
Their voices rise,
human voice mist, a silver casualness
thrown back into the dark.

2

What hides behind the dusk?
Light-sluice from another world,
down there at the end of the west-facing block,
only orange shards point the way, cairns on the journey
to the looming mountains, the blackness beyond tree line,
larger than an open mouth, as large as the turtle's journey
as he drags through the wet sand to the river.

The fading light is inside you.
All the times you have been alone rise from the blood,
the orange wisps of solitude swirling around inside;
light lifts off the earth, finished;
everything finished.

A lone swing in the park.
Cold metal chains and a wooden seat.
The skin listens for its forests
as your feet scrape along the scooped-out dust under you.
You push up and out in the metal-squeaking dusk,
farther and farther out, parallel with the tops of trees.
You long for something friendly,
peer into the swinging disappearing earth
like a duck flying north
toward the long-absent marsh, the swerve back into earth waters.

TRAPPED

1

We drink wine,
sleep in the sun and look at the blue smear of the river far beneath us.
Later, I walk past the edge of town,
out along a country road where red-winged blackbirds live.
An old man is putting in a garden.
He has gone in for lunch
and planted one glove each on two sticks of his picket fence
and his hat on a third.
My hands are balled into fists
like the woman in the blue coat
walking so purposively,
her hands pointed straight out before her,
as if she were blind,
stumbling through the thickets of air.

Back in the city, spring multiplies in a drunkenness of mud and water,
the houses with high fences like barbed wire,
sudden whine of a siren turning into a shriek,
the mother who shouts, "OK, fifteen minutes!"
The mother who shouts, "Now!"

Sometimes five senses are not enough,
not enough cups to catch the rain,
the bodiless voices from open windows,
wind shifts,
new grass cracking open the dead earth.

2

Walking the prison yard on the first spring night
Doug said, "Remember street lights,
how they cast a shadow?"
We looked past the old wooden gun tower
to the Missouri fields
ploughed into the blackness; and there too, the red-winged blackbirds
flinging themselves against the last light
beyond the prison glare,
almost brushing the fields
as if they were a second, wing-tipped, horizon,
moving so fast as to be barely visible.
This is the wilderness beyond the body's last border
where the old man puts on his garden gloves again to grow fruit in the
    prison, the world.

SECRETS

for my mother on her birthday

Somewhere at this very moment someone is eating peanut butter right out of the jar! He is alone and the television is off. His mother has no idea what he is doing. It is his secret. Very far away a dog barks, a horn honks. The day his grandmother died he had a crazy desire to laugh and yet he was very sad. You don't tell your mother your secrets for fear she won't love you.

FOR A MOMENT

I stood deep inside a willow and found it better than love.
I saw a willow's heart. It was green and easy to touch.
For a moment I was a willow-animal.
Anyone could touch me deep inside. I was easy to touch.

IN THE NEW WORLD

I am not sad to come back.
The inner world gives me bones—
they form themselves in silence,
they ask no questions.
They dance, they have patience.
They measure the round in years.

When I come back from the bones,
the pure fish that moves in the wind
and that has no desire;
when I come back from the pulse,
from the breath, from the belly
that delights in itself;
when I come back I am not sad.

One by one
I entered the world. The circle
of the world. My friends,
my enemies, all the streams
that needed my weight
to fall inward once again
the falls I became
poised over nothing.

This is why there is no sadness
when I come back, I come back
to this: my friends and I hold hands
in a circle. There was music,
we hurt one another,
our bones called *need,* our fears
danced before our eyes,
our sex hardened,
there was no more water calling
only salt
on salt.

This is why there is no sadness.
I lick your tears,
your salt writes our names on my tongue,
our rings of salt mean forever.
Ashes cover nothing, sadness is not,
even the salt turns inward
and falls through the sunlight.
They say, *oh, the salt, the sea,*
but no, it is not that, not happiness,
not sadness.

from

THE FREEDOM OF
HISTORY

(1988)

TODAY'S MEDITATION:
"IT'S NOT SUPPOSED TO LAST FOREVER"
Cavafy

Every day, and for no apparent reason,
I remember prison. My footlocker,
barbed wire out the window, how coffee tasted—
instant, lukewarm from the bathroom tap
first thing in the morning. I would stand there
sipping, watching the Standard sign through the barred windows,
miles down the road. I can still see how red
that sign was in the pale sky at dawn, so far away
beyond the fence, and yet near somehow.
I stood next to the shaving mirror,
as close to the sky as I could get.
Even then, I knew how lucky I was
"and I really lived in undivided love."
I understood how the loneliness and the love
would always be mixed up inside me,
like a sky and its Standard sign bound
together in the little nearness of time.

TODAY'S MEDITATION:
HAPPINESS

In the end,
all that matters is light and dark,
and what's not finished between them.
As long as he stands back far enough, deeply
enough inside the room, he is fine, he gets
the point of things: how they come, then must go.
But the blue sea beyond the window: it has
always done this to him, always forced him
further into happiness than he thought he could stand to go.

TODAY'S MEDITATION

He went to bed early, and dreamed well.
Wild sex, many secret meetings.
Toward dawn, he woke as usual.
That is, he felt somehow guilty
for the pleasures, the dark secrets.
He noticed the leaves, and took heart.
They, too, had had a wild night.
They were yellow and shriveled, barely
hanging on. As if they also had loved furiously,
secretly, and now were in a state
of shock. It was a new day, and all
over his country men and women were making coffee,
putting on the shirts and pants behind which our bodies
lie still all day, sleeping like owls, worn out
from the night's long chase, its bloody victories
and secret, unremarked defeats.

TODAY'S MEDITATION:
TRAVEL: RAVENNA

I thought we came here for the mosaics.
But really it was to ride this bus
with an old man on one side who smiled
and an old man on the other who frowned.
Really, we came here to see
the yes and the no creased across the stubble
on two men's faces: the one way
a life of ecstasy,
one way a life of absolute denial.

Here in Ravenna where a mighty empire
began and ended near the sea,
two mighty camps
still meet daily on the bus,
the empire of yes and the empire of no.

Nearby the mosaics shine with the impersonal delight
of those whose lives have been resolved as art,
their dark-rimmed eyes already inducted
into eternity: so far away can the yes and no go, so
beautifully can the empire be shaped
into cut and glittering stones.

This, then, is our present: to chart
the past—obscured, dense—
already ascended into the heaven
of finished things. Meanwhile,
the yes and the no make themselves at home inside us,

relay their secret messages back and forth
like children who refuse to be silent
at a funeral, death so near they could
reach out and touch it, but life—its thousand
urgencies that must be whispered *now*—
even nearer.

A SUMMER AFTERNOON, VENICE

You feel how good it is,
this earth, sitting on the cool bridge
made of shadows
that swings between pine tree and church.

Pigeons search through the dry grass,
diligent, working their turf.
If, at 44, you begin to learn
you are not, after all, the point of the world,

what then? The bells ring 6 P.M.,
shadows no longer just a bridge,
but a road widening into darkness
and the night beyond. Everyone

is going for a walk on that road
one time soon, if not here
where the roads are made of water,
then somewhere else, somewhere equally strange,

some tide-lulled Venice of the brain.
There is a moment when our empires fade to nothing at last.
Where once we had stood ashamed,
unable to understand our place in the universe,

now moonlight is there, shining its bridge across open water.

TODAY'S MEDITATION:
THE CRUCIFIXION
Tintoretto

It's still going on.
It's not even close to being over:
the man in pain hanging there, he
hasn't got a prayer. He'll go slowly,
he'll take hours. This isn't
about God, it's anyone who's going down
inch by inch and won't be coming back again:
there's not a thing we can do to stop it.
For centuries, this has been happening:
someone dies slowly, alone, without comfort.

No wonder the sky is black behind the dying man,
and the fern's a sickly green
and the ground is a dusty unforgiving slab
of cracked earth. This is where we live
and the only God to believe in is the God
of Suffering, the man or woman bound hand and foot
on the cross of whatever pain has finally claimed them.

Here's what we do, Tintoretto says, we who live on this earth,
who watch from the sidelines.
Some of us ride fancy horses, pause
a moment, gape in horror, then
gallop away. Some of us are poor,
are on foot. We, too, stare, we, too, leave;
but more slowly, one step at a time,
looking back in fear, we can't
help ourselves, such suffering. Some of us
point. With our right hand we are saying,
look. But our heads are turned away.
We know we need to see what the world
is doing to one of its own, but we can't bear
to really look. Some of us hide

in dark corners: the ones who have cards and dice.
Bottles that are almost empty
guide some of us through the darkness: for us there is
nothing to see, nothing to look at, all suffering
is a distant smear of paint, beautiful in its way.

There are always a few among us who gather
at the foot of suffering. The humble ones,
usually the women, the mothers,
the ones who love not because it is right,
but because they must. In this collapse
of women in beautiful robes next to two men
who believed in him, in this collapse
called grief, in this sorrow
beyond endurance that is—
in the name of love—endured,
in this collapse of the faithful onto bare earth
begins what Tintoretto sees as the only peace
that is worth painting, the one
that lives like this, sprawled at the feet of suffering.

It is the rest of us who sadden Tintoretto:
how busy the painting is with all the ways there are
to miss the point of our lives in the face of such
incessant, unceasing mortalities. There is no justice
such suffering could possibly serve. And far in the background,
one ghostly figure standing by herself
on the left, surely a signature
to all the rest, a pure creature
of imagination, solitary in her flickering,
insubstantial body, blessed
by the absence of life, the absence of death.

THE FREEDOM OF HISTORY

(1980. Prague: the Iron Curtain still firmly in place.)

1

It is a spring night in Prague. A man in a park in his mid-thirties and a woman,
twenty years older, are sitting on a bench they've pulled over to a corner. This
way they can see the river and the Charles Bridge. She speaks:

These beads are too big: amber
from some other century when necks
were larger. I think my whole body
must be a sack meant for that century.
I'm six feet of awkwardness and the beads
look like carnations of melting butter on a string.

Don't turn away. I won't talk
about myself now. It's so easy
to feel sorry for yourself with a man
who listens as you do: your whole body
leans toward me and my English
is a secret between us. I have no one
but the children to speak it with now.

Everything you hear in Prague is music
because you can't understand our language.
It is a wide river that washes slowly around you. Or,
(how I love metaphor at night
with the chestnuts in bloom and the blue
electrical flicks of the trams across the river;
and you inside that white shirt)
you stand on the bank of a strange music:
the language reminds you of nothing
but a waterfall, a pillow of sound . . .

No, don't turn away. I won't talk about you.
I know you came here to forget
how to explain your life. We drank
a toast to that in white Moravian wine,
though the Germans
at the next table were so loud we had to shout it.

I'll explain history
the way the city taught me.
But wait. Did you hear that?
An owl. The first I've heard in years here.
It must be by the old water wheel over there.
I love creatures. Now that they let me translate
from English again, I do books
by veterinarians about the pets
they've restored to health. That owl
is wild. I must tell
my daughter. She'll want to name him
something human and pretend, she, too,
wakes up at night, watches the city
with feathers at her sides.

This is the city at the center of everything.
(White blossoms of the horse chestnut
fall in your hair.)
Europe runs us through in every direction.
We have no ocean, no horizon
we can look into endlessly. We have
no distance to lose ourselves in.
For centuries we have built this city
to be our ocean. This is why the buildings
peel in pink layers of stone:
they are waves slowly finding a shore
in the century before them, beneath them
in the layer before their own. You know
the silence old people drift in and out of.
Attention bores them. They'd rather
open a door into a courtyard and see

a girl standing in sunlight: she holds a brown pitcher
filled with beer brought from the corner
for her father. Or, they'd rather turn and twist
and be a narrow road winding up a hill
toward a magnificent castle, black and shadowy
against the blue powder of a spring day.

You've said the city pulls you
and you don't know why. I want to read you
what my husband wrote when he first came to Prague.
It was fifteen years ago. Things were different then.
There was a sort of freedom. (You don't
have to look around: it's safe.
We look innocuous, like lovers.
No one would guess that what we say
might matter.)

You are wrong to turn away like that.
I'm not talking about me. This is him,
like you, a stranger. He, too, was sick
of himself, of all the questions, the decisions
to make that never seemed to matter. He, too,
wanted an oracle. Like you, he came here on impulse.
Those ornate combs he gave me for my hair:
they were meant to turn me regal,
piles of hair and a determined chin! Anyway,
he was young then too, and English
to his toes. He came here to meet my mother,
to see the city where we might live
and learn to translate one another's languages.
I brought the first letter he wrote after he left.

"Prague is like a dream, more so than any other city I've seen. It's so
odd and so filled with that old life. Archaic—suddenly that word, its arch-
like sound, takes on life. The arches of the archaic.

"Prague is not a museum, not an artificial arrangement of fragments
from a culture. It is a whole; people live there. The city has a life of its own,
separate from any one individual's life. It all grew so slowly, it all moves so

slowly now. It is not a city geared to efficiency or to a known goal; but to a journey that can only occur in streets that twist under arches.

"It is a city built before capitalism and through a strange twist of fate still preserved from it. There is little 'exchange' there; much drifting and wandering. Its solitude overarches one's own. It is not a city desperate for the personal exchange, whether of money or relationship. Things take their course. You wander. The city catches you up, just as a dream does. There are no companions when you dream, you always do it alone. It is a city which grows in power at night. Far from feeling excluded at night as you do in any large city in the west if you are alone—exchange grows even more desperate in London at night—you feel even more embraced, more included. The dream grows more vivid.

"I'm not being romantic; it's worse than that and more dangerous: it's a-moral. It's a-contemporary. The city of Prague is a kind of music, the only art which represents nothing but itself. It is a world that will be endangered the more often I come to Prague. It is a world that will end entirely when I learn the language: the more I understand the 'real' Prague, the less music I will hear."

When we lived in London for a year
I loved the Tube most.
Late at night, the smell of cinders
and stale electricity. The buckets
of sand. And the old men
who wait for the last train.
Have you seen how they look
straight ahead at the wall of the tunnel
opposite them? (I am too elegant in this dress.
It's so long, so green, puffy in the sleeves
like a mushroom rotting in the bin. I wore it
for you. Because you're from New York.
I should have known it was wrong:
elegance, even out of date,
is not what you came for.) They wear
thick coats there, the tweed is smudged,
their hats . . . anyway, it's late in the Tube
and the posters have begun to peel.
The tunnels seem ancient then, burrowed

into a mountainside. It is quiet.
London seems miles away. It is the closest thing
London has to silence, to the arches,
to the centuries that have hollowed themselves out
into Prague.
All of the west is one big shop.
There is nothing for you to do but make decisions.
Prague is a city
without decisions; without choice; the centuries
tell us how to be silent; the state
tells us how to speak. But I've said it wrong.
Inside the silence, an owl hoots:
it makes me want to ride the broken water wheel
round and round in the silent night.

She stops speaking. They both get up from the bench and walk to the low wall that separates the park from the river. It is very late now. The smell of horse chestnut blossoms everywhere: that strange mixture of freshness and rotting. He wants to be alone. They agree to meet two nights from then in the Slavia. Her high heels—somehow she manages to walk in them as if they were boots—slap loudly on the cement. He looks for a moon, but can't see one.

2

The Slavia is a cavernous old coffee house. It faces the river almost opposite from the Kampa. They sit at a table facing the Hradcany, the castle which dominates Prague. It is lit up. All around them people smoke, drink coffee, talk, and read the newspapers. She speaks:

So, you came. You want
to hear more. But first,
look around you. What bird
do the people here remind you of?
I see the dove everywhere I look:
so much gray in the jackets,
in the felt hats and sweaters.
So much bending and cooing,
poking at cakes, whispers, gossip.

Sometimes I think we'll all grow wings
and fly into the past. Live in a belfry
or on the edge of a flying buttress
from one of those centuries
that you have come here to rediscover;
maybe you and I will be doves together . . .
but I forget; you say
you've had enough of metaphor:
you want the truth.

Have you noticed how the centuries collide?
Romanesque, Gothic, Baroque; they never stop
running into each other. And yet,
when a person walks, say Karlova Street,
it's impossible not to feel it as logical
as a bedtime story a father tells his children,
a fairy tale in which everything belongs:
owls in water wheels, horse chestnuts
blooming in a man's hair, a woman
whose husband died in a crash in London.

Forgive me for being personal.
I can't help my life. It collides, too:
our own century and our lives. The truth
you want is lying under stone.
The Jewish Cemetery.
It's so old
no one has been buried there for hundreds of years.
The graves have all collided;
stone is stacked on stone.
They buried their dead in layers,
century after century. Now the stones
are dug up, so many you can hardly walk
from grave to grave. These stones
are the new grass, the meadows
where this century has learned to graze.
Isn't death our architecture?

So, you see now, I am not alone.
I am a Jew.
My metaphors keep me company.
I don't blame you for wanting
the silence of our streets, the anonymous
architecture of a city that has stood so long
in spite of everything. It's good,
sometimes, to wander like Kafka
in Italy, or you, here. He needed
so much: the sun, the hair
of women. You need . . .

(Don't turn away. I won't tell you
more than you can hear.)

My little girl wants to be an artist.
She likes to draw spires and roofs,
the tops of things. I come home
from work and there she is,
cross-legged on the window ledge.
She loves to look.
When she's tired at dinner
she watches the grain of the wood
in our table. She's cold
in winter. Here's a poem
someone her age, her race, wrote in '42 at Terezín,
a concentration camp for children:

> ". . . those thirty thousand who are sleeping—
> Who shall awake one day
> And shall see their own blood shed around.
>
> "Once I was a child—two years ago.
> My childhood was longing for other worlds.
>
> "But I believe that I'm only sleeping now,
> That I shall return with my childhood one day,
> With that childhood like a wild rose,
> Like a bell that calls one up from dreams.

". . . What a horrible childhood that decides for itself
That this one is good and that one is bad!
Far away in the distance my childhood is sweetly sleeping
On the paths of the Stromovka Park:

"Perhaps one day I shall realize
That I was only such a tiny creature—
Just as tiny and unimportant
As the whole of that choir—
            those thirty thousand."

He didn't know that choir would reach six million;
for me, they never stop singing.
And I have seen the German tourists
eat their sandwiches sitting on the stones
of the dead in the Jewish Cemetery.
Do you want more truth?
Forgive me my anger, my irony.
It's rare to speak in English,
to find someone so unknown
to history as you are.
Tomorrow, I'll show you
a garden with the mystery
my husband loved. The Slavia
is no place to forgive wounds.
I told my daughter about the owl.
She wants to draw it; but the eyes
stop her: those rings. She keeps
circling in the shadow of his sight.
I wish I hadn't told her.

3

The afternoon is sunny. They meet at the Waldstein Castle. She guides him from there to a garden two blocks away. It is on a steep hill and it is a long walk to the top. She speaks as they walk. At the top they find a bench where they can look over the roofs of the old town and the city.

Here's where the secret begins,
the space anyone needs who wants
to look at things carefully. Veterinarians
are all the same: they have
their favorites they speak to
repeatedly, but who never answer
in the fawning language of the pet.
Artists, philosophers, priests, veterinarians—
those who look repeatedly at the world
and try to understand—need such an animal.
In Prague these secret gardens are our unspeaking
but attentive beasts.

Here's where we sat. My husband
loved the roofs from up above like this.
They have the comfort of a quilt,
the old American ones
that took years to make: jagged squares,
unpredictable, crazy; but held together
by the care and dreamy absorption
of the ones who sewed.
From here, from this secret place
that holds us and does not speak,
I see the quilt whole; not separate patches
but the centuries sewn together into the tiles
that cover us all. From here the city

always looks asleep under the dazzling haze
of red tiles in sunlight. From here
the city never stops dreaming. Last night
I dreamed you were one of the secret police.
You wouldn't let me photograph my city.
You wore that brown sweater of yours,
only it had turned to armor. You smiled,
then broke my camera. You said,
"Lincoln is my hero,"

Yes, turn away. I don't blame you.
I think you were my husband
trying to return young again
to warn me against the images
I love. It is dangerous to stand
in a secret place and look down on the city
where you live and say of it:

this is a dream. It's dangerous
in the secret place, with the lilacs
and bridal wreath blooming sweet
and acrid. It's too perfect
with the wind on your back
in a high and hidden place. You begin
to see for miles; far beyond the quilt
covering your own life, beyond even
the hundred spires that rise from Prague.

You stand in the secret place and you see
the flood of distance, the shimmer
of the unknown. It never stops, that slow
movement, the third, in Beethoven's *Hammerklavier.*
I saw a Hungarian play it once;
he, too, was beginning to go bald
(no, don't be embarrassed; the head
becomes more powerful then, as well as silly).
He bent to the keys
as if looking for something
between the smooth ivory fingers. He lifted
his own fingers so slowly: they had become weights
that could barely move through the slabs of ivory
as he looked for what was lost
in that landscape of granite and winter:
flooded fields, bare trees, and the light
that only distance gives to snow.
Have I gone too far?
Isn't this what you wanted:
to be inside the curved panel

of a God's landscape, a smudge
of color far off in the corner
of Monet's largest water lily?
It was for this that my husband worked
those long nights in London
when the rain is a blanket
unraveling its endless fibers in the yellow light
of streetlamps. Here, too, the nights are long,
distance as impossible to measure as the childhood
of one who dies at birth. Distance, dusk, the owl
that sleeps under the steady eyelashes
of a young girl's careful looking.

4

She is alone in the vinárna *called* The Golden Hat. *She sits at a table waiting
for her food. As she waits, she thinks about the young man who has left now to
return to New York.*

How much I forgot to tell him!
But men are different.
It's so easy to bore them. Still,
I think he would have liked
the cucumbers on the white platter
they serve here with a little salt.
And the Camembert sprinkled with paprika
and white slivers of sweet onion.
It is always so silent,
the walls thick, curved like the wine cellar
of a monastery centuries ago
when history was a dream,
not a dialectic. But the dream remains
inside the dry Moravian wine. Tourists
don't come here. I've never heard German once.
Only the composer
Smolinik goes out of his way to sit here
drinking wine. All he does
is revise now, old work

from the war years.
It is easy to sit here for hours
with the wine, the cool walls, the silence.
Nothing seems to happen,
as if we were monks sunk in prayer
in the deep dream of a god whose need
for our devotion never stops.
It's almost 3 o'clock. My little artist
will be home soon. Then dinner,
and afterward that silly book
about the pet beaver to translate.

Later yet, long after the neighborhood sleeps,
I'll walk in the narrow streets beneath the castle.
There'll be a moon tonight. I'll do ten pages,
then walk. I need my city to myself.
I won't let my city regret me.
How many moons I've seen
hang for a moment over the castle.
When no one's looking late at night
I pick lilies-of-the-valley
from beneath the castle wall.
Such a tiny flower, such small white bells
to be ringing in the moonlight
beneath all that stone. I don't need him,
that man—I'm not alone—I have my eyes
which don't belong to me, but are two
amazing friends who keep opening for me
onto spires, Camembert, and the moon.
I'm not alone. When a tram car
flickers in the distance anyone sitting
by the window is my friend. He sways
with tiredness and I sway with him;
he turns toward the beautiful woman
two seats over and I understand.
We are always afraid, but never stop looking.

I am alone with all the others:
the ping-pong table beneath the frescoes;
a boy leaning his head out the window of a wall
centuries thick to call his friend across the square;
a mother pushing a baby carriage; a grandma
carrying a solitary orange as if it were the sun in a string bag
to her boy, the night porter at the hospital.
I know them all—
the Russian woman no one has spoken to since '69
who puts out her patches of laundry each day
hoping a neighbor will finally take pity and speak;
and the other woman who cries
if even a squirrel should die;
and, oh, the lives of the men
glimpsed through the wooden doors of the smoky taverns.
They stand behind their tall glasses of beer
and look through the golden windows of those half-liters
into longed-for garden paradises filled with fat carrots and televisions, roses
for their wives in blue jeans and lipstick;
and the cool night air in which no one is screaming.

It is here, in these lives, all of them, that the city
honeycombs the thick centuries with the breath of the living,
with brooms and feather ticks, with buckets
full of soapy water, school satchels and sweat,
until the centuries grow light with the porous breath of life
and are swung up over the backs of the living like so many sacks of laundry
carried into the future where their clothes will be worn again
shining with the heat of the freshly washed,
put on as if for the first time ever.

WINTER SMOKE

As if, simply because we were born
we earned these tears,
this sky, those manes of wild light
galloping away behind the black branches of our dying world.

SNOW

1

It is silent forever in this new world,
calm, and falling whitely.
I am the slow falling,
dropping, dropping.
Breaking up the sky,
I become its length and breadth,
the unmarked thickness across the windshield,
an evenhanded emptiness
breathing in like the baby asleep in the new ship
of its untried body, breathing out in the shape
of a snow-driven man, still sailing
the white drifts of his own quiet breaking.

2

Snow's depth is the instant shape
it gives a thing: what snow touches shifts,
just slightly, bringing the sweet pleasure
of merest change,
the way a human will touch a human
lightly on the wrist and that day
is different, slightly and forever.

Like snow, I was born
in the distant belly of a mother
I never knew as well as when,
point by lovely point,

I was forming myself inside her.
I came from nowhere,
fell softly on new air.
I did not know where the drift of weather
or the iron tide of chance would carry me.
I fell far beyond my own control,
giddy with release.
I was most myself
in this my only falling
onto our earth.

DETAILS FROM THE AUGUST HEAT:
YOUR RAPE ONE YEAR LATER

The unripe tomato left to sun
on the garbage can lid, the tight
yellow wax of its waiting, the ground pitched
sideways, unbalanced, its sickly green
looks weakened, the color of a lime
held under water. Slick with August dew,
this day must also begin for you.

One year ago today, you woke, in darkness,
to a new, less complicated life. A knife
at your throat, a man unbalanced, slick
with that addiction: not to you,
but to your life, submerged, blurred
beyond all recognition. Not to you,
but for your absolute, unwavering attention.

Tiger lilies have a way of hiding out
against garage doors, brick walls, or a gray
fencepost. My old landlord keeps them for his wife,
dead three years. To whom he sings each night,
playing badly on the mandolin. Music
is at least a fan: the sorrow pushes
at a curtain, touches a face, rearranges the invisible

helpless air. "Well, now you'll have
something to write about," that young man said, then
raped you. "Details," you wrote me once,
"those are the things which can be said,
huge and neglected." The next day
you left that place for good. You found a house
with double locks, a yard, a suburb far away.

And then the nights began to make you pay.
Terror is boring, each night the same ritual:
he is back inside the house, making his way slowly,
cut by cut, into your waiting life. You are certain
that you will always wake like this, forced
to be what he must have, again and again. His face
will never end. His jittery way with words. His steady, gloved hands.

The old man has a secret: water
every night after dark. A pool of black water
under each stake. He says
that's what it takes for tomatoes *like this:*
he makes a circle gesture meaning perfect.
Perfect is a full night's sleep.
You will lean up against it, a gray fencepost,

and one night it will hold.
This day waits for you, huge and impossible
to neglect. You will not forget
where you have been and what was done
upon you. Details from the August heat:
grapes ease their way from green to purple, you
work all day then turn to children's stories.

Once upon a time, the large print reads,
and the words glide by
like illustrated days in a bedtime fairy tale.

HERE, TOO, THERE IS A PARADISE

on a photograph of Prague by Josef Sudek

If the city has a bridge, he loves it
in black and white. Streetlamps and statues line
the Charles Bridge side by side. The old tide
of night is coming in, rising in gray
streaks off the river. Each statue is a saint
face on. As if swept bare of people,
the bridge stands pure and expectant.
Colors are not permitted in Sudek's world,
are unforgiven for their gorgeous pandering
to reality. This is something else. Here,
in this landscape of black and white, here, too,

there is a paradise. As Prague approaches
night, each black shape on Sudek's contact sheet
calls to the other. This is what love is
on a bridge: the dark of one shape calling
to the dark of another. Streetlamps, saints: all
the smudged and haunted ones. Sudek searches
his city for the moment when gray sings
to gray, and river to bridge; when all things
resemble one another just enough
for statues of saints to light our way
like streetlamps, and for streetlamps to speak
to God like saints, with the gray light of unlit
glass faces. It is almost too dark to see
the clouds above Sudek's Prague, where already
night moves among the restless, unfalling rain.

ROTHKO

He saw the gray on black, and that
was that. Two shapes of dark
came at him, parted, waited.
Shapes had been like chairs before.
He could always rest in a shape.
Before gray came,
every oblong was a way to say the world,
a pitched tent of color in the wild
and arbitrary forest of all our longings.
He even found his own Matisse,
his homage, in oblongs, like a window
thrown open on yellow and orange, on patterns
that only the casual eye, lazy with joy, can find.
Sometimes he dreamt the world pastel,
dreamy curtains of color he hung
over bars of light, and left to be opened.
But he couldn't drench the black.
So, he painted what he owed it: square
after square. He gave the black
that final gray, a last oblong weight,
the simple and furious grave above the black,
the last place he had to go to paint. It was
hardly dry, but he went in to stay, inside
the shape he had made himself of himself.

MATISSE'S *DANCE*

Nothing we do will ever be as free as this:
outflung bodies tipped toward blue sky
like ecstatic toasts about to be drunk
by an earth that can barely contain them.
Never looking back, the women clasp hands
as they dance, scatter the invisible air
with buttocks and backs, sheen-black hair, unclasped
and comely as Stravinsky's sad Petrouchka, freed
at last and laughing. They're never going back
to clothes, to elastics that force stomachs flat
or rein in breasts; nor to gravity
that weighs us down like sacks of wasted flesh.
The unresistant green of a painted,
slippery grass lets them leap as if the earth
is a trampoline, a paradise
of jump and whirl and touch. Up close, we see
green paint streaks their legs like a spring rain.
It leaves a careless, splashy wake, an ex-
uberant trail of jagged, squiggly clues:
this is the dance of those with nothing to lose.
They go round and round, splashed with paint,
and covered all over with a thick coat
of pleasure. So absorbed in the wild fling
of their bodies, their lowered faces
are solitary, monastic, filled
with the godly pinks of shiny flesh
defying gravity on the trapeze
of its dance. No net, no pole, no need
for balance at all. We who remain grounded,
bench-bound, watch their flesh shine, delicious
sowing of blue leaps, green robes of cut grass
channeled in a flow of color deep enough
for us to drown in. We who breathe
must have these small deaths by color, leaning
as far as we can into the river

of pure astonishment. We hoped
paradise would be like this, so much green
spilled into blue, everything unbuttoned
from gravity, naked, dancing hand in hand.

TERROR'S ONLY EPITAPH

On December 29, 1975, a bomb exploded at LaGuardia airport in New York in the baggage area. Scores of people were killed or seriously hurt. No one ever took "credit" for the bomb; the guilty person was never found. At the time of the explosion I was waiting for a plane one floor up and a little to one side of where the bomb went off.

I

I saw how it was with the living.
All the sudden conversations,
little spurts of talk
springing up like campfires
at which we warm our hands:
"Three dead?" "Three,
hell. Twelve at last count,
and still digging."
"My God.
My God."
The words
keep us warm.
We never give our names
as we talk.
We all have one name:
survivor,
and each word we say
is an added degree of warmth taken
from the raging fire
those twelve voices
lit for us.
A blue light in an ambulance.
Like a grotto blue in a da Vinci
it is the center around which
death huddles.
Again and again, the ambulances come.
The dark blue lights shine, add
darkness after darkness
to their glow.

A young boy sits on the hood of a car
in the parking lot.
A bag of Christmas presents is at his side.
He cries, and is ashamed.
He bends his head to the sack
to hide his tears.

We found taxis, did knee bends,
ate grapefruit. I saw that it was easy
to go home: the arms
of a lover held me tighter
than all the arms of the twelve dead.
It was easier
to see the dawn of the next morning
than to stay one more second
in that broken night.
It was easier
to return home
than to stay a stranger
among the dead.
It was simpler to speak
the old language of the living,
than to learn the bloated
and indistinguishable syllables
of those whose mouths
are full of dirt.

II THE DEAD ONES SPEAK

Try to see how it was.
We've just walked down some stairs for our baggage.
We're thinking of the trip around the world about to begin,
or of the next painting we want to do,
or we work for the Long Island Limousine Company
and we've come to pick up the bags of arriving passengers.
We are chatting, we grunt under the bags' heaviness,
secretly we curse all weight.
Or we are remembering the left-hand corner

near the frame where we might put in a dab of black.
We are not forgetting the suit that must be pressed,
nor the course we almost failed,
nor the orange dress that packs so well.
We think of that old teacher who died in Mexico last year,
and the raise we didn't get.

Something was just on the tip of our tongue
when glass—which had been so smooth,
which had always opened before our touch,
which had given us light
and through which so much world had entered us
as we stood at windows or lay back with the shades up—
when glass which had never spoken a word before
enters our ear with a little whisper.
Or it speaks to our throat
and our head sails across the baggage area
(like a baseball, says a witness later)
or it pushes everything it has against our face
which hides in a thousand places
and won't come out and isn't ever completely found
before the funeral.
Or there's a large hole in our jacket (how did *that* get there)
where once there had been a stomach.
Our bodies became a kind of rubbish.
Here a hand, there a shoe, here a head,
there a hat. We had no plan
at the moment of our deaths.
Don't try to say we were brave,
we never had time for that.
Don't try to say we were special,
we were ordinary as breath.
"Heart-sickening," a survivor said later
of what was left of us. Heart-
sickening is the only epitaph.

III IN THE EVOLUTION OF TERROR

At first,
when a universe is created,
God has too much to do.
There are already widows
who must be comforted.
There are wedding rings
without any fingers
because the bang that created
this universe spared rings
but not fingers.
It preserved metal
but let the flesh go,
brushed it off people's bones
like lint.
It was casual,
this bomb—
without pretense
or false politeness.
It took a druggist,
an artist,
an old woman.
It specialized only
in drivers of limousines:
three.
In the beginning,
God invented the parking lot.
A universe of concrete,
of people milling in small groups,
of fist fights over who used the telephone,
the one telephone
God had installed
in his parking lot.
In the evolution of disaster
many strange creatures appeared:
ambulances with blue lights
revolving in their white interiors,

sirens that never stopped
and men in blue uniforms
guarding the new universe
with drawn guns.
But the strangest creature of all
is the dead.
God invented the dead,
12 silent and unyielding disciples,
before he invented dying.
He gave them their deaths
before he taught them how to die.
And then God rested.

IN RAIN

Only the gray cat crossing the silver of an empty street.
Only the pigeon picking at its breast,
fascinated with the perpetual itch of its own body.
Only sex in front of the fireplace, the old
hesitations, the flames a blur
of creamy light on the ceiling.
Only the me and the you, the thorn and the rose, the hurt
still falling and falling though the cat is easy
and swell, its tail tipped in white.
The how of its stroll through the sky's dripping
is only one truth, but I want it. The fur
slicked back along my body. And the naked.
And the who that glitters within its bullet-shaped head.
It is only the sex. But I want it. And the how and the who
of the world's tears falling everywhere at once
and me the one with the red tongue, rough,
a rippled muscle drinking, only drinking
at the trough of the sky's fallen body, those tears, that sweat, our rain.

WHAT THE BIRD SEES

You rise up in the darkness,
over my body.
The white necklace at your throat,
the balls of ivory around your neck.
You open
your water-lily flesh
high up the side of the mountain in its own pond,
swaying, unafraid.
The blossoms rise small and tight
out of the green lips of the palmy leaves.

Need has found its breasts and entered them.
You invite me;
the leaves of your blooming are wide and wet.

The motionless bird on the chimney flies up.
It saw something there in the distance,
maybe another blackness like itself,
maybe the soft curl of sticks and hay woven in the circle of a nest.
The weave of darkness, the ivory beads, the sticks and hay
of our mingling breaths. We saw what the bird sees
and bore up our separate wings to that waiting nest.

GIVING AWAY LOVE

Since morning it's been raining on the sea,
since morning it's been graying. Herons
scrape slow shadows across the flats.

There are eyelashes in the morning, little feathers
of seagrass caught between rain and the saltier rain
of the sea. I am darker than the rest, and dry

like wood under a tarp being saved for the fire.
The truest dreams have rain for faces, have surf
for their long rolling bodies. They don't wake,

stay dignified and a little crazy. They
rarely stray this way, so close to waking.
But since morning it's been raining on the sea.

I say that I'm dry, but I'm on the edge:
a little balcony with an overhang, feet wet,
barely awake, giving love away.

Inside the room behind me, still
in darkness, sleeps the woman I love, a dream
away, before us the slowly forming day.

I'm giving love to the sea, a wing, some grasses.
Giving in to rain, and that shifting, wind-drenched
gray. Giving in to dreams I can't remember

and a certain dryness: this flimsy body something
lives in called "I." Giving love a flowering and a need:
since morning it's been raining on the sea.

LONDON: 33, THE LAST MOVEMENT, THE LONGEST DAY

1

He was 33 for the last time.
It was late afternoon and he'd seen the tailor
on the museum's wall with his black scissors and row
of perfect buttons. Then he'd gone to the large room
with the awful reds and sunsets laminated pink
and stared at The Four Stages of Man
and their objects: toy, guitar, armor, money.

Each stage was gloomy, and so, to cheer himself
he stopped in room 24 at the laughing cow
in the della Francesca, its mouth gigantic with blue
in the otherwise dignified and eerie whites
of the nativity scene. It was London, June '77,
late afternoon of the year's longest day and his last chance
in his old year to stand next to a cow belly—
laughing with joy at the virgin birth.

The deaths of Christ in the medieval pictures are silver,
a moon of flesh stretched across the canvas, light
by which to see the world bathed in death, the staked planet
of the body on the cross: orbiting god
of deep crevices, dark side, valleys and mountains.

2

It was 5 P.M. when he left the museum
to walk a while in the gray light of Saint Martin's Street
past the sidewalk portrait painter. The man
who was barely 33 thought of the gauze on those christs
of the 14th century, the translucent silver cloths,
the dead penis under its gauzy map of the crotch's wilderness.

Every few feet he stopped and made a painting in the air
of what he saw before him: lovers standing
by a trash basket kissing until the news vendor
who also sells concertinas turns away.

The man walking alone on the eve of his 34th year
ate his cold green pepper,
drank Scotch and coffee at the place where the Woman
Who Sits Alone dines in the splendor
of her notebook, pen, and books spread across the table.
If only she knew it was his last day on earth at this age,
maybe she would turn from her dreamy pause, pen in hand,
to answer the many questions for women he has formed
at this and all his unknowing ages.

3

He has chosen for his last evening at 33 the concert
of Beethoven's last sonatas, four shells
washed up on the last shore,
where those forms that gave his life shelter
broke with the passion of age and regret.

The man in the concert hall was afraid to put the shells to his ear
for fear he would only hear the echo of his own longing.
But there it was, faint at first, the ocean,
that deep wind-entangled water of our birth,
those first floating bars of the opus 101, A major
that depart so quietly from the silence which precedes them.

The man has known since 4 P.M. that he is trapped
in armor, life's Third Stage, head
propped up by hands at the painter's insistence
on the truth of posture, of a body inside armor
where shades of gray metal frame the exposed flesh of the face.

This man who is losing his year at last
is able to find the music of Beethoven's last years
by the final sonata's final chord
in that solitary moment when the pianist is ash gray
as the flesh of the thieves on either side of Christ.
In that silence when the player's fingers tremble over the keys for the last time
and do not move again into the ivory flesh of the instrument's body,
the man who has been completing all day the portrait
of his visit to the kingdom of 33
relinquishes it into the open palms, the wild
applause for this final, difficult, and unfinished music.

ALL THE RAISED ARMS

The city wanders in spirals
from market to cathedral, from museum
to gutter, from café to postcard.
It takes its time and it pauses
at the flapping blue laundry, it puffs
its pipe at the signpost: the Divine Lily
is coming! Who will return
Lost Kitty of 8/15? The gray eyes
of the steeples are always so calm.
Part of the sky is a forehead
and part is the vague gesture
of an old man who lost his hair
and has walked all the way to the edge of the city,
crawled over the stone fence and separated
carefully the weeds from the flowers.
He puts the bouquet by her name in the little cemetery.
It is blue in the sky where his old hair
has blown far off in a corner. Someone took
a wheelbarrow and gave it to a little boy
right this minute, right now. He turns
its wheel with the pure exhaustion
of his play. He is moving silver
to the castle behind his mother's table.
His shirt is blue. Two tourists
have been given noon, a paper bag
with cheese, bread, and a little butter under a chestnut tree
full of the dust of Europe. Bells, wings, the worm
of a day is catching a quick nap behind the white grandmother curtains
of the house on the right. And that silly bimbo of a grocer
has gone off again with his rolled sleeves and his bottle
looking for God knows what along the path behind the convent.
The spiral turns inside the rolled newspaper of the housewife.
She is looking for flies who have dared to invade
her kitchen. All the raised arms,
the stifled yawns, the winks.
All the open mouths demanding their bread

and singing their songs. All
the years that marbles have crashed against each other
inside the circle by the school. Not one is lost,
not one. Even the headmaster turns
and stands by his window to watch the game
and is not lost.

THE POET OF MINSK

(Russia, 1928: in memory of Mandelstam and the others)

The ice is melting in Minsk. Mid-March, the smell of black earth,
ice-stars under the streetlamps. There is a certain tree
on a certain corner where the buds open before all others.
The poet of Minsk knows this and much else.
What it means, for example, to love streetlamps,
which coffeehouse you can sit in for hours undisturbed,
which secret police (they follow him now day and night)
allow him to dangle on a longer rope, will let him
enter a store without following closely.
His friends weep for him. They forget whole lines of his poems.
It is hard being the most joyful man in Minsk. He sees laundry, squirrels
on the dead tree, Spring like a velvet tam on the end of his fingertips.
Why settle for one year at a time! He looks at the old man on the corner
and becomes what he sees. He turns toward the angle of roof beam,
where the pigeons roost. He is a pigeon, a roof, a beam, a dark strip
of pigeon world. He is a dead man. He knows that.
He is the only statistic in Minsk that stands alone.
No one who loves to murder would pass him up.
It is a beautiful night,
says the man who was pigeon, old man, piece of rotting wood;
a night like all the rest, wonderfully like all the rest.

FOR YOU

I know it sounds too much like poetry,
but it was dusk that made me a felon,
a winter evening in Moline, Illinois.
The next day I quoted Whitman
to my draft board, "Dismiss
whatever insults your own soul,"
and sent my draft card back to them.
I can still feel the cold metal
on the mailbox, see the park
with its oaks, the black winter sky
so close, so distant,
as I dropped the letter inside
and turned quickly away.

For two years I'd argued the War,
drinking instant coffee with a man
who wore the same blue velour shirt so often
it's all I remember of him now.
We took turns arguing one way,
then another about "what to do."
We sat in the basement kitchen
of a boarding house.
Sometimes we yelled,
sometimes we sat silently, our hands
around our mugs of coffee,
our hearts confused. Deferments
from the draft meant we were the men
who could afford to choose a future.
And we had so wanted to go on drifting,
floating on the moment's shifting current
as we learned to give the poems we tried to write
a chance to rise, waveringly,
into their own shapes, existences
born of dreams, not arguments. I didn't want
to chant slogans. I didn't want
to be "right." To judge.

And these were more than choices,
these were entire lives, futures
that could never be redeemed—
or so we felt then in the midst
of a slaughtering time.
Back and forth we went, the guy
in the blue velour shirt and I,
all of us who read Emerson and Thoreau,
ate frozen dinners, drank
3.2 beer, played pinball or pool—
any game at all that would give us
a few hours away from ourselves,
those of us who underlined
CIVIL DISOBEDIENCE and wrote excited comments
in the margins late at night,
rather than actually take to the streets.

I lived alone in Moline, Illinois,
one dusty and dimly lit flight
above a greeting card shop
run by a likeable red-faced
John Bircher. It was the first year
I got paid for teaching, paid
for being excited
about what I believed in,
for having opinions
I couldn't give away
to my friend in the velour shirt.
Then two students quit school
and within months were dead
in Vietnam. A working class
college, our basement classroom
was in an old pentecostal church.
The mix of Sunday School
and poverty was too much
on Monday mornings, the students
almost asleep, sprawled
on the freshly waxed floors,

huddled near their classrooms
like refugees waiting for their morning soup
rather than for classes to begin.

I was the razzle dazzle guy
from the Big U
in Iowa City. I didn't
own a tie, I lived
in a VW bus all fall,
I had opinions that gave off
the glitter of newly minted
funny money. To the students
I was a classy eccentric
and I had them with me from the first,
those future postal clerks
and nurses, mechanics
and would-be writers
with their mixed bag of Sartre
and letter jackets, hickeys
and acid and—finally—
of life and death.

The second student who died
had sat in the back of the room,
chair tilted against the wall,
his long hair spread out behind him
like a scraggly fan. He often
brought his guitar to class
in a black case, and wrote his poems
on cheap yellow paper. He wanted
to know about mileage
from my bus: these
were the only details I remembered
when his girlfriend told me he had been killed.

It was winter by then
and I was living alone
above the greeting card shop.
After that second student's death
I spent the weekend by myself.
I was reading Suzuki at the time
and wanted to believe in something,
even if it was only the pull
and release of my own breath
as I sat cross-legged, meditating
best I knew how. I liked Zen.
For someone raised an Anglican
it seemed the closest thing
to all that upper class tastefulness, so
lovely, so earnest in its own careful way.
While I sat, meditating, I felt
even lonelier: all my enthusiasm
in the classroom, my voluble
and spontaneous love of poetry
that fit itself so nicely
into the 50 minute school hour,
my a la mode hiking boots.
I thought of that dead boy
with his guitar and his questions,
and the careful but wasted economy
of his cheap yellow paper
and I felt sick to my soul,
for all my talk of Thoreau and Whitman.
I wanted to be a citizen again, to Pledge
Allegiance to something with the faith
I'd felt in 4th grade, facing
the flag behind Miss Rodger's desk.
It was my country, too,
not just the John Bircher's downstairs
with his saccharine greeting cards
and his private gun collection.

That weekend I drank green tea,
believing it more Japanese than Lipton Orange.
I stared at the gray clouds
of dust under the bed, I followed
the flow of my breath
in and out of my stomach—
like a golden river, Suzuki said.
For two days I did nothing
but alternately sit and then hobble
on legs permanently sore
from being crossed so much.
I quit thinking about everything: the draft,
my dead students,
the future, the past. Was it
a spiritual state? I don't know,
but I felt as if I'd grown 3 inches overnight
and everything I saw
looked slightly different,
smaller and further away,
the way a dream does
as you wake up
and it begins to leave you.

Toward evening of the second day
I'd had enough of the hush,
pause, hush, of my own breath
and the shooting pain of ankles
and knees. I wanted out
and away from those motionless dust balls.
It felt wonderful to walk into evening
alone in Moline, Illinois,
in the middle of America,
the weightless center
of a centerless country.

I walked and I looked.
I saw some men sitting at a bar.
I stood outside, staring
through the small pane of glass
at the top of the door.
Everything moved so slowly:
my breath still deep
and even, holding me rooted
in the evening air like an anchor
when men fish from a boat and seem to drift,
but are only rocking back and forth
between one known place and another.
I saw the men, heads bent
toward the neon light of a beer sign
behind the bar: a man with a lasso
in one hand and a beer in another.
The lasso was red, the beer golden.
A bartender stood beside the sign,
white-aproned, holding a pencil.
I watched as he gestured
toward the bent heads of the men
sitting before him. One of them
nodded up and down and that simple,
barely noticeable sign of agreement
brought tears to my eyes
and an assent of my own
where I stood anchored
by my own steady breath.
I walked on, went up the hill
that rose steeply away from the river
near where I lived. A sled
had been left out for the night
on a front yard's thin crust of snow.
I saw this ordinary sight
framed in a deepening gray
like a letter in a phrase,
still undeciphered, but so important
that once I understood it
it would change the meaning of all other words.

As I walked slowly up the hill,
other objects I saw seemed part
of the same phrase:
a porch swing drawn up on its two chains
waiting near the roof for spring;
a car with a broken windshield
glittering under a streetlight
like the traces of a phosphorescent map;
the corner of an old newspaper
frozen into an iced-over sidewalk.

"For you," I found myself saying
over and over as I neared the top of the hill.
My breath came in short gasps now,
"For you, for you."
It became a kind of greed.
I couldn't get enough
of the men with their bent heads in the bar,
the sled, the swing. They gave
and I took.
I wanted it to go on forever,
this greed for the world. I knew
that it was for the sake of a sled
left behind in the moment of impatience
for dinner that I would go to prison.
Not just for political reasons,
not even for moral ones:
not for reasons at all,
or not the kind I could explain
to a draft board. For you,
sled. For you, bent heads.
For you, for you.

If, in a moment of peace, the world
could yield up such signs,
then I wanted an inner peace,
both permanent and casual.
But I could not begin
until I settled with the War.
It was that dusk, that walk, that sled
that convinced me their world could sustain me
if only I could abandon my soul-searching
and endless arguments over what to do,
like a character in a Chekhov story
so busy talking outside
on a cold winter's night
he almost dies of frostbite
while trying to prove the existence of God.

If it meant going to prison,
so be it. There, too, there would be
ordinary sights that would sustain me.
Or so I told myself
in that moment when I believed so deeply
in the strangely calming power
that came from seeing clearly
into the heart of everyday life.
I stood at the top of the hill, alone,
surrounded by what I loved.
I looked down toward the Mississippi,
black except where a bridge curved
through the night, and I did not know
what the future would bring
or what it was inside me
that would not let go
of my two new words, "For you."

from

THE LONG EXPERIENCE
OF LOVE

(1995)

THE LONG EXPERIENCE OF LOVE

(on being photographed while holding a photograph of my mother)

I can see right through her to the world
beyond the porch: a single bird
of paradise and two scaly palms.
When she could still see well enough
to care about shapes in the world,
gardens were the pleasure she most loved
to work. She is almost weightless
in my hand and keeps shaking,
though I try to hold her still,
so that others may see
what I see: a guardedness that cannot hide
the unmasked plea for love passed down
from mother to son.
Our lives are small things,
easy to miss. The truth is
they do not belong to us at all,
but must, in the end, be returned
to the sky: to that same mottled distance
so like the speckled blue of the bird shell
I found when I was six
and she was thirty-four.
It was broken, that little suitcase,
and the dried and wasted shine
of a fallen life was stuck to the shell.
How I cried then
because of the litter a death makes
when it falls into our world
for the first time. I raise my mother
to the day's last light
for fear she might slip away
into darkness before I've had enough
of looking at her. My mother pretended

to love that broken shell
as much as I did
because this is what mothers do
when their children cry out to them, undone
for the first time by a world in ruins:
they make it seem natural to love what ends.

QUEEN ELIZABETH ON TV

It was my first look at the world
on a small screen: her coronation
in my aunt's living room. It's amazing
how close I came that day to loving
what I saw without question. A small boy
staring at a queen. Both of us were excited.
Both knew it was crazy how things happen
beyond our power to understand them.
The queen and I, we were enchanted: earth
and all its glories seemed enough. Have pity
on us, we who would have loved to rule
our whole lives without incident. We who
have spent our reigns dissolving empires
into warring nations. It was in black
and white, a tiny screen, but it was godly
how she walked down that long aisle alone,
only her heavy train behind her, only
her failing empire before.
We kings and queens cannot help our accidents
of birth: born to rule, born to lose it all.

TO WISH IT GOODNIGHT

Though my father complained
of the grammar nurses use
when they help take you
out of this world, the truth is
it was not ain't that made him angry.
It had once been so easy
for my father to simply
get up out of a chair
and leave any room he wanted
to be done with.
I saw his eyes follow me
suspiciously, as if it were betrayal
for someone so healthy, his
only son, to walk freely
in and out of the small white room.
But he tolerated the way
I just had to reach
down under two sheets
and touch his foot, a thing
already buried so far
as he was concerned, useless
thing with toes.

He wanted to go on awhile
being my father. Instead,
at 7:24 A.M., he sat up
for the last time and retrieved
one more breath from his thinning air.
He whispered to those of us
who continued to breathe
without even trying,
"She's finally
coming." Then he lay back
to wait, then died.

That night I dreamt my father
took a nap.
Just as he was waking,
the dream ended,
and I, too, woke.
Together, we both left
for our next worlds,
his newly assigned,
mine the same old sunlight,
morning joggers and blue sky.
How near we were
in that dream: he
on the white couch, I
in the brown chair watching
his lovely, clouded eyes open
onto the world.

In life, he was not nearby.
Now he is
everywhere I dream
and every place I wake.
Or if not him exactly,
then a nothing
so much like him
I cannot seem to wish it
goodnight, when I try to sleep.
In death, how completed
the absent one can become.
How easy to lean forward
in the brown chair
and stroke his thinning hair.
And death is simply a sentence
that he has just spoken:
but only the beginning
of what he has to say.

During his last days,
when there were tubes for everything
that left and entered
the body, and the nurses
couldn't help but wish
my father was gone
because then he would have been
happier, during
the last days,
I turned on the Cubs
for my father, so he could see
one last failed run
at the pennant.
After the final out, I
approached slowly
from the left, speaking
clearly, my grammar perfect.
I offered him a grape,
and in this way, I gave my father
his last food by hand,
something small and purple,
as beautiful
as it was useless.

AFTER MY FATHER'S DEATH

Almost a year later, from a train near Innsbruck,
I saw a woman about his age. For a moment
I glimpsed the half-hidden bench where she sat, her face
turned away from the passing train, all that speed
and purposefulness. Her dog slept nearby, its head
under her hand. She sat very straight, her back
against the slats of the bench as if it were a pew
and she staring at the man who dies so slowly
on his Cross. "Sacred Conversations" is the phrase for paintings
that embody her wordlessness, her calm moment
near a meadow, haloed by snow and ragged peaks.
The people in these Sacred Conversations
stand silently, looking down and away from each other, united
by devotion to what they cannot name or fully understand.

My father and I almost stepped outside
our separate frames and spoke our love. Instead, first one of us died
and then the other took a train that passed near
the woman, her sleeping beast and the silent mountain.
Who knows, really, why a father and his son
must sometimes spend whole years together, not even
looking at each other. As if a third presence,
perhaps a dying God, demanded their linked aversions,
a Sacred Conversation instead of something
profane, born of this earth and their own small time together.

THE YOUNG MEN

My father, naked in the photo, young
again, crouched among rocks and water. It's an island,
a time so long ago he is thin,
buttocks tense with the pleasure
of climbing down toward beach and sea.
Who is this man who so loved sunlight,
bare skin? Somewhere inside
all the fathers
are these young men:
virginal, unburdened of thoughtful,
mysterious sons and stubborn, principled daughters.

I have the photo to prove it:
they are climbing down rocks
toward the sea. They are almost
on the beach. They are naked
and happy, filled with delight
to be crouching on the coastlines of uninhabited islands.

THE PORTRAIT

You want me lying down and I, too, love the unbuckling,
the slow lowering, alone, onto the old green couch, eyes now
barely open. The camera stands stiffly on its tripod,
a kind of disciple in need of focusing from
someone like you who fusses over sleepers and serves
the world by preserving loss, one image at a time.

At first I track you as you move above my body.
Stretched out near sleep, I am the helpless universe you need,
someone about to lose himself to dreams, to disappear
beyond any purpose or hope a waking world can solve.
Alert and intense, you hover above me.
Meanwhile, I fall asleep. For me, it's just another nap.

This time I'm gone longer than usual. When I wake
you've moved the gladioli behind my pillowed head.
Arms crossed over my chest, I feel refreshed and calm,
as if, waking at my own funeral, I find that death is simple,
not like life at all. I lie still and wait for you to finish.
It's love that lets me trust you with my sleep, arrange my death.

Death brings out the best in me. These portraits help me see the soul
I might have been, set free from useless fears. I see a man
I forgot I knew, someone subsumed by stillness without
regret. I wake to see myself as you do, a calm one
at rest, a little dazed, still posing from his sleep, as if
first comes the letting go of life; and only then, the wakefulness.

HOLD UP WINTER

Hold up the tree. Hold up the world
as well as you can in heavy wind. Find a friend
to help you. Hold up the skeleton, a photo
of bones in black and white. Hold up
the core of the world with bare hands.
Hold up the map, the route from tip to branch,
trunk to root. Hold up for everyone, the core
beneath the leaves, the totem that is hidden
under abundance. Hold up winter, that shivering truth,
the season that refuses to bloom. Hold up
the memory of another time. Try to obscure
the present, to distract it from its wish
to rule the world. Hold up the blueprint,
the soul of the tree. Don't stand too close
to the world as it seems. Back up, then look up
into the bareness of things before they learn
to hide behind their green. Hold up the image
of what remains, even at those final times
when all seems shorn of life. Remember
to wish only for what you need. Hold up
the simplest tree of all; a totem woven from light
and the barest of branches. Hold up—
here in the windy, green-leafed present—the memory
of what once was simple and bare, of what
did not require us to hold it still as it grew
silently, and with purposes of its own, on the empty hill.

TRY THINKING OF DEATH THIS WAY,

as the landscape within which the finished body
is one more incidental: as rocks are,
and moonlight, as dark pines and the white
filaments of a few clouds in the far distance.

BOY

(A sequence of poems written to an imagined son)

1

You would have found my chest
without even trying, and under
each of your arms
I would have found you. Boy,
you would have had the perfect black hair
of your mother, but those blue eyes
would have been mine,
mine, mine.

The doctor picks you up afterward, after
the long journey, and it makes you cry
to arrive here, in this world.
Because you have already worked harder
than you will ever have to work again,
you are wrapped in a clean white cloth
and laid in your mother's arms.

On your first night,
I would have held you
up to the window,
as if you could see the moon: you
who only hours before would have finished your work
as a tide. *Moonlight,*
I would have whispered in your ear,
then carried you back to your crib
where you would have fallen asleep
again, even before I knew I was saying
welcome.

2

I never wished you anything
but a father
when the darkness comes,
that and hide
and seek at dusk:
there is no
happiness like holding out
alone in darkness, hot
and sweaty, waiting
to be found, your
whole life ahead of you.

Darkness
understands best by feel,
the way a glove does,
taking the fingers one
by one, emptying them
of touch.
Darkness
is where light lets you go
when you need to be
alone, a place
beyond explanation, even
to a son. But you
already know how I love
what can't be explained:
you.

3

If you had been born
into the nearness
of a body, the scent of an actual
specified flesh, if you could
walk beside me in the sand,
you would see for yourself
the heaving spirit,
the pooling flesh
of the sea,
and I would not need to say
the obvious then, how it
roots and teems in
our blood, mirrors our souls
in the ripped lair
of its invisible depths.

Sometimes I can't stand
how ceaseless you are,
how ready
to come back to me again
and again, wave after wave
of you almost
existing. Like the sea,
you are always ready
to begin again, and like the sea
you never give up. You are
that shoreless thing
inside me, ripping
and soothing. Just as you
would have had a thumbprint
all your own, so the sea
is a signature. Don't
even think of counterfeiting it,
you'll never get it right.
Let the sea sign its name
to our lives, since everything
about it is teaching me
how to miss you.

4

I tell you what I've told no one
because you don't exist
and because you are so deep
inside me: he worked
my nipple with his fingers
and everywhere he could harden me,
I did. Can you believe it,
fifteen already, and I didn't know yet
how good I could feel
just because someone knew
to pour cheap champagne
into me and then where to put
his hand?

Once surprised like that,
you never forget your body
owns you. You are its toy,
and it spins you
out of control. You never
forget his name, the one
who rubbed your face
in pleasure, who betrayed you
into need. Then,
boy, it is dawn
and my blue pajamas
are back on again, the name tag
right where my mother sewed it,
so as to avoid any confusion
about what goes next to my skin.

On the morning after,
I open the curtains,
then the French doors and stand naked
from the waist up in first light.

He keeps sleeping
behind me on the bed, his
ankles so white, like roots
upended and exposed
to the sun.

The very idea of morning
then is beautiful to me. My life
is in ruins, but I don't
see it yet, how yesterday
I had been a boy and now
I am one no more. He began
by teaching me Shakespeare,
how to trust what is foreign
to the tongue. Only afterward did he take
my penis for his own. "I love you,"
he said and sent me out into the world.

After he finished with me, his hands
nowhere in sight, I drink white coffee
from a white bowl, then ride
the bus, my new secret life
curled up between my legs.
When I leave the bus, there are Matisses
in the white house on the hill
near the place where a boy
in a black mask and cape keeps
riding his bike in a narrow circle, chanting
Zorro est arrivé. Inside, there are
odalisques, so cheap looking,
so dark eyed and available, I
want them, they could be me
all spread out like that, waiting
to be used.

5

After him,
I would let nobody
touch me but myself, and then
only under heavy sheets
of running water, when all alone
I'd coax my erection
out of hiding and no one
was there to make me regret
the small cry
I gave at the end.
When you think no one else
can stand to touch you
but yourself, if you will
let me, I'll rub
your back from the down
of your small shoulders, all
along the knotted spine, that
abacus where shame
strings itself along
the body. About kneading
the small, unviolated back
of my son, no one has a thing
to teach me.

6

Maybe what you want for me
is to move away from you.
Alright then, I can do that,
I can love a thing that actually
exists. In the spirit of what might have become
you, I lift my eyes to the body
of the city. I watch how
it clothes itself in darkness
as dusk turns into full night
and I remember my mother
bending toward me in black
velvet, red lipstick, perfume stuck
to her flesh. How excited I was for her
that she was leaving,
for one whole night,
the son who could not give her
happiness. I look
into the city's darkness
with the same love, expecting
nothing, as I once looked
into my mother's darkness, the same
look you must give to me, you
who can expect nothing from me,
as I bend toward you, nothing except
the perfume of existence,
which cannot help but cling
to everything I do.

THINK OF THE WORLD AS A WEEK ALONE

As if someone said, go, then you went,
and this was what you were given: a night
at Saint Martin-in-the-Fields, a long evening
with the next-to-last of Beethoven's quartets.
You tried to listen as if listening
were all. But in that interval between movements,
where Beethoven intended only silence
to accompany the intense and fussy preparations
for the unfinished music that lay ahead,
shouts and screams entered from across the street
in front of the South African embassy, whitely
chaste like an untouched wedding cake.

Think of the world as a week alone in a strange city.
But think of it especially as this one night
when after the concert, nearby at Trafalgar Square,
two women stood together, oblivious
of you, and said their good-byes.
The one getting on the bus was in tears.
The other, older, more sure of herself and stronger,
said, *pray for me.* Then, in case
it wasn't absolutely clear, said again, demanding it
calmly, *pray for me.* The other had no choice
in the matter. Then,
just as you were sure it was over,
she leaned out the window to her friend, *I*
love you, she said, and it was so unbearably true
the three of you each stood a moment, stunned, not thinking
of what had to happen next: that the bus must take her away.
The demonstration was fading, hundreds of black balloons
had been released in the name of a freedom
that exists somewhere: if not in this world,
then surely someplace nearby.

When the 24 arrived, you sat upstairs,
a moon on your left as you moved up Charing Cross
and took the long way back, Camden Town,
Highgate, and all the rest. By the end of the route,
you were famished. At the Curry Paradise
they put you by the window, but you'd had enough
of the world for one day. It was time for a postcard
to someone familiar, someone from your other country.
Think of the world as a week alone, you began to write.
On the reverse was Keats's House.
You could have walked there after dinner
if you'd wished, could even have stood alone
in the darkness under his favorite tree, the one
he wrote of more than once. But you didn't
want to push your luck too far.
Think of how you just happened to appear
this week and no other, at the exact moment two friends
said their good-byes overheard by you
who had nothing more important to do, not then, not ever,
than to stand like that in the middle of such parting.

Think of the world as a strange city,
only partly yours. Think of it as silence that should have
let you rest between movements, but didn't. Think
of it as black balloons released into a blacker sky,
as a moment under a famous tree
that almost happened, or as the plush paradise
of a dark booth: spiced and unfamiliar food. You were so hungry,
and this is the meal you wanted, the one you needed to eat.

WITH TIMMY, IN AND OUT OF PRISON

1

From the very first, Timmy and I were a pair, each of us
with our curly hair and bushy sideburns
cropped close to regulation length, each of us
with our hunger for words with more syllables
than we would ever need. College
and degrees, textbooks and research papers, were as exotic
to Timmy as his Kansas City—full of good luck
and bad, fast and dirty, desperate and black—
was to me.

Timmy was proud and quiet, stubborn
and easy to offend.
I never learned what he had done
to end up in prison. There's an etiquette
about such things: you don't ask
and are rarely told. Men in prison seldom speak
of where they've been or where they are;
the future is the only place to be.
But I kept waiting for him to tell me,
to sit me down one night after yet another
macaroni and cheese dinner and say,
"It was like this, see. One night
I got a little too high and . . ."
But that conversation never happened.
Nor the one about our pasts,
or the secret hurts
we had carefully nurtured
for years. Instead, we talked about
the easy things: Marxism, modernism, ecology,
theories that would solve the world
of our fears. At the time, it seemed enough.

2

We looked through magazines together,
especially the ones with pictures
of a countryside in full seasonal bloom.
We paused long over Vermont trees in fall,
over cold mountain streams slowly warming
in spring sunlight, or winter birch trees
drifting in several feet of cresting snow.
We looked at them the way a traveler
looks out the window of a train
passing through beautiful countryside,
mesmerized by what our hands could not touch.

Timmy and I decided to write essays.
His were always on Africa, ancient tribes
that meant little to me. How carefully
he bent over the white page, pencil
in hand, his eyes so close to the paper
he seemed to be examining it
for defects. Together we made a language
of our love for ideas. We wrote
with the same longing with which we watched
the seasons change in the pages
of those glossy magazines we loved.
No one has ever
demanded more from theory than Timmy.
Some people have a taste for questions,
for living in ambiguity; but Timmy needed answers,
explanations of the world that would hold.
He'd lived with enough unanswered
and unanswerable questions
to last a lifetime.

3

My white friends said we'd never make it.
His black friends said the same.
But fate had given us
a shared captivity, this strange mirror
in front of which we could stand
and admire our own sense of possibility.
After all, this *was* 1970
and we believed in change as if it were a god
that could do us no harm.

One evening we thumbed through the magnificence
of Victoria Falls, turning
the pages of an old *National Geographic,*
Timmy shaking his head
at the immaculate blacks in crisp whites
staring down at all that falling water
from behind the guardrail where they had transported
the equally awestruck, equally crisp-looking whites in their care.
"Man, you and I shouldn't be looking
at all these happy niggers carrying luggage
for white dudes. They're setting a bad example
for you. Don't you think I'm going to take you
and your suitcase to any waterfalls
when we get clear of here, my man."
He laughed but there was a tension
lurking behind the easy joke
that marked a boundary
we had so far avoided crossing.
Then we both yawned and called it a night,
happy for each other's company,
though nothing of significance had happened
unless you could say getting through one more day
in that place was in and of itself a sort of triumph.

4

Maybe it would have gone on like this indefinitely,
the pleasant monotony of friendship
in a place with so few pleasures.
But one afternoon I forgot for a moment
that happiness was dangerous in prison:
it made you forget where you were.
I decided to visit Timmy in the laundry room,
where men shouted over the hiss and smoke
of huge silver machines that tore at the dirt
in the wrinkled pants and shapeless,
unloved shirts. Timmy and I could be
friendly apparitions together there
in the midst of all that steam, forgetting
for whole moments at a time the prison
that surrounded us on all sides.
When I came in that day, Timmy
was bent over a laundry cart,
sorting clothes. Since I didn't know
how to touch a male friend whom I loved—
the easy movement to arm or shoulder,
or that quick brushing across hair—I snuck up instead
and gave him a light kick on the butt
as if we were both kids in college,
male freshmen in search of their adult lives,
yet willing to take time off for adolescence
with friendly pokes in the ribs and mock-angry grabs.

Timmy whirled when I touched him,
keeping low, his stomach protected to avoid
the knife he assumed his assailant
was about to use. Then he rose up

into my stunned face, his left hand
already shaped into a fist, his right
at my throat and open, the way a claw is open
when it is about to slash.
I understood instantly
that my life was at his mercy.
He saw that it was me
and pulled back. But slowly,
as a partner might pull back
after a dance he is reluctant
to see end. "Don't never,
ever, come up behind me like that again.
You just can't *do* that."

A few seconds later, he apologized.
But in that instant when he had been
at my throat, we both saw the distance
crackling between us, palpable and spiked,
a current that we went to elaborate lengths
not to touch from that day forward.
We let up after that on the home-brewed beer
we used to share together in bitter little sips,
let up on the way we checked in daily.
I was sad and angry, but mostly confused.
I had no idea what to do.

5

I gave him my address
just before I got out. We imagined
our first reunion
in his Kansas City, or maybe
at a pig roast in my green Iowa.
Even then, I think I knew
we never had a chance. Within three days,
"Here Comes the Sun" was all I could hear
as I danced in the living room
of an Iowa farm house. My eyes
were closed, my entire life
ahead of me, and now
I could assume the next moment
in a way that Timmy never had
and never would, in
or out of prison. I was free
to turn my back on anything
I wanted. I was home in my America.

"Here Comes the Sun"
was a whole other life
and I tried to live it as long
as I could. The failure
of that music is another story,
but in the meantime I was twenty-seven,
three days out of prison and already
Timmy was as far away from me
as those scenes in the glossy photographs
when we'd sat on a bunk and imagined
Summer, Spring, Winter, Fall,
beautiful weathers unfolding page by page
for us in an America
even I knew did not really exist. Already,
our life together no longer seemed real.
I didn't know it yet, but the doors
of a different prison had just swung shut.

And that should have been the end of it.
Except that a year later, he called.
He was finally out, too.
His voice was low and cool, far away.
He wanted a place to stay for a few days,
and could he come visit? He needed
to "get away" he said and laughed.
I heard a little of the old Timmy in that giggle,
pleased with himself to have found
just the right words. I was afraid, but said, yes, sure,
of course, man. Hey, it'll be great.
He said he'd call when he had the flight number and day,
but he never did, and I never heard from him again.
I was relieved. Then ashamed
of that relief.
How quickly he became for me
one of those beautiful small towns
profiled in the glossy magazines we'd loved
in spite of ourselves, a stylized happiness
so full of hope it seems exotic now, unreal, barely
of this world at all.

6:30 A.M., THE SOUNDS OF TRAFFIC

The man who was my friend
is my friend no more. When the light
finally comes, I too, will find my place; I too,
will sit behind a wheel and steer.
When we are gone from this earth,
who will care that my friend and I fought?
Soon enough, I will fasten my seat belt and turn
on the news. As usual the world will be a sad
and dangerous place. To whom, then, will I speak
of this sadness, of the danger that is everywhere?
To whom, if not to my friend?

JANUARY 1, THE BEACH

The daughter wears a long T-shirt.
She's four at most, in search
of the shallowest wetness she can find.
She already knows "no,"
and "careful now." She already
believes the warning about a bad world, a wave
on top of a shark on top of an over-
your-head mindless tangle of salt water
and sea wind and going down forever.
The whole point of the game is to hold
a plastic bucket as a prop and skip
to the edge of the world as she knows it.

Her older brother is short-haired, pale, intense: he's just
too busy to waste time on her. His work:
to order the most excellent and perfect shells
to come toward him out of the surf.
She would scoop them up
in indiscriminate fistfuls. His passion
is for the perfect glistening shape,
wet and gasping for air like a face
under tears. One at a time, as if shelving
expensive delicacies, he places them in his pail.

Mother's butt is on the blanket,
her toes dug in under shells and sand.
Her wandering glance refuses
all loyalty: she looks from magazine
to horizon, spends more time
eyeing her nails carefully
than watching her children.
The delicious sag of her body
says it all: she's on this beach
for the laziness. Let him
do it this time, the first
child watch of the day, the year.

And he does do it.
The husband and father stands behind
his fishing pole, not watching
the line for fish at all, instead
tracking the T-shirt-enveloped
four-year-old and the serious boy
of ten. The pole is his prop
and he holds it toward the water
like an offering.
He keeps jerking his head
back and forth, as if trying
to look in all directions at once.
It's how his whole body keeps stumbling
against the surrounding air
that tells me this trembling
is unending. It goes
where he goes. It is his only home.

The fishing pole shakes
in his hand, and his hand shakes
against the bulky, unstable shore
of his body. At night, he must stare
at the place where darkness pools
on the bedroom ceiling. Does his wife
just lie beside him, her stillness
a kind of reproach, his right hand
on her left, working the space
between his body and hers?
Or does it matter
as long as their skins shine together
in the velvet clasp of flesh against flesh?

When the fish strikes, not one of us
is ready. The woman jumps to her feet,
the girl shrieks as she runs
toward her father, the boy

lets his pail fall and all of us
watch the man at the slippery task
of bringing it in. It's a beauty, too:
silver, huge, flailing away
at the universe of air and light.
In the moment of surprise,
as the fish leaps, the man's neck
forgets to shake or jump. He grows
as still as a concert hall
in the long moment after the last note falls
into silence and everything is solved,
momentarily, before the applause.

It is time now
for me to go home. The show is over.
The family on the beach stays behind.
They have their fish
and their day at the shore before them.
Later, I will go to the grocery store
where the young woman works
whose baby died. She decided to stay
in this small town by the sea.
"That way I'll always know the names
of the streets where he would have walked,"
she said once when I was leaving
with my milk and bread. "Thank you
for listening," she said as I left.
As if her grief and her love were things
she'd owed me, a kind of debt.

PREPARING FOR FIFTY

for Mary Rockcastle on the occasion of her 40th

It came to me that I needed a valley.
It came to me that I was done with the salmon
as my totem, how it scrapes its way upward over rocks,
how the body quivers and strains, as if waiting
to be touched for the first time. All that is fine
for thirty, even forty, but for two years now I've believed
in fifty, someplace where who I am counts for more
than who I might become. Last week at long last,
I found a valley where I could be the small thing
for once. I could lie down in the hot springs and just be
covered. I swayed there in the water and waited
for the calm that becomes a body at fifty.
It came to me how to be at home on my back,
my genitals floating above me, an obscure species
of water lily drifting back and forth,
hardly attached to the long and clumsy root
of the body. Soothed and silenced by water, it was here
that my life has brought me, wrinkled as the day I was born.
This time around I was calmer, more sure
of how water and earth work together to offer me up
to the valley. As if I were a human sacrifice,
given up in the name of love, baptized in water, flesh
and blood in the valley of stone until the last breath.

THE TASK AT HAND

(downstairs neighbor)

My friend who is afraid peeled an apple
under kitchen light. I barely paused
on the back stairs, going up with laundry,
and saw a woman overwhelmed by the lacks
that have begun to collect themselves:
the deaths of friends, an older sister,
the grandchild born too soon.
Then there are the sudden cancers
on her skin, one like a blind eye,
red and empty of all purpose, blistering her forehead:
as if she were a worshipper who had tried to scrub it away,
no longer believing in sight by mystery.

I woke this morning and thought of you, my friend,
how the night before you were standing by your sink,
attentive only to the task at hand
as you worked the apple to its opened flesh.
If only we could see ourselves
as the momentary souls we are,
almost finished before we have truly begun. Surely
we would have such mercy on ourselves
that even our griefs and fears
would become part of the work that feeds our souls,
that devoted attention to the task at hand
wherever it may lead us, that *is* our souls.

IN THE CAFÉ: THE GROWN DAUGHTER

Suddenly the daughter puts her left hand to the forehead
of her mother. As if to mark the furrow with the cross
that only love can bear. As if she is the priest
and her mother the penitent. She tries on
the mother's sunglasses. But they are too large
and there is so much darkness behind them.
Then the mother begins to speak. The daughter sighs deeply,
inhales the bitter smoke of a cigarette,
as the story unfolds for more than an hour.
Finally the daughter pushes away
from the table, pushes away slowly
as if it is the smooth body
of a lover to whom she says at last,
no, enough. She leaves. The mother looks around
at all the tables where no one sits whom she loves.
She looks longest at the girl who reads alone
at the counter, absorbed in *The Diary*
of Anne Frank. For a moment it seems as if the mother
might interrupt the girl. But no: what, after all,
can be said to a child lost in the story
of another's life? Streetlights come on. The mother
puts her sunglasses away. Now it is time to smile good-bye
to the man behind the counter. To look at the girl in love
with the girl in her book. Nobody interrupts anybody: the story goes on.

FRESHMAN PAPERS

Like orange candy wrappers, writes
the daughter now, describing the time
years ago when the goldfish
were thrown into the street
after her mother died.
Like litter, but still
trying to swim. And then,
there's the young man
whose father flew over Hiroshima,
just afterward. My student wanders
around in prose until
he discovers why his father never speaks
of what he feels: *Maybe he saw*
too much death even before
I was born. The son tries to forgive
the father in paragraph eight.
Title: *My Father the Stranger.*

If I only had
one mistake to take with me, red pen
in hand, into the grave, I'd choose
surprise: those misspelled words that drop
the undeserving reader
without warning into *hys-*
terical, rather than *his-*
torical, or it's a *doggy*
dog world. And truly, it's a dog
eat dog world. Take the daughter
who just last year
remembered the neighbor's zipper
when she was six, then seven, then eight,
how it scratched her cheek, how carefully
he dried her face.

Daily,
I spoil their terrors
by pleading in the margins
for more or less.
I grade what I can and leave
the rest to them to revise
as they must, these sons
and daughters with their lost subjects
and ruinous verbs, their bent heads
just inches above the paper
when they write in class,
free hand cupped around the words they form
so that no one will see before
they do, how it is their lives
turned out, now that I have asked.

NEAR HERONS

1

With the sun a full inch above the horizon, comes
the wind. The old man, becalmed in a white shirt, stands
with hands in pockets before the world's freshening,
the water in the bay beginning to shrug and shiver under the spur
of the raw, still unsettled light. Think of them, old men
all over the world sliding on their shoes in the dark,
by feel alone. Old men who do not wake their wives,
but step quietly out on the grass or sand
and stand in a place where they can see the sun
rejoin the world once again.

2

It is my pleasure to think of the men: my need
to see them facing open water near herons,
ordering nothing to happen
in these, the last days of their lives.
Near herons who know how to leave earth for miles
at a time. Creatures who, when stirred, open their wings
without a sound and lift themselves into another world.

IN ROME, I RAN THE TIBER

It was dawn in a great city
and I was a grown-up in short shorts,
out of place and a little frightened.
Not a soul in sight. The Tiber
churned wide and deep beneath me,
as I crossed a bridge and took a hill.
A baby cried.
I looked in all directions for an infant
left by the road at dawn in Rome,
until I heard another, then a third.
The cries were floating down from above.
Angels? It was Rome, after all,
and there was nothing frantic in the cries.
But when I looked up, I saw a dilapidated,
sprawling hospital, the maternity wing.
And then, before I knew it, all Rome
was below me, hundreds of silver domes
slipped inside the watery smoke
of day's first wavering light.

I might have stopped right there,
but then I would have missed
the merry-go-round and the two women
in white smocks—they could have been nurses
on break from the hospital—who ran it.
The music was on and the horses,
riderless, were rising and dipping.
The women watched me expectantly,
as if, perhaps, I had run all this way
to be the first, so that I might have
any horse I wanted
and ride in splendor
in a small circle high above Rome.

Somehow I missed my turn
for the hotel and ended up, alone
and panting, at the Forum. All
I'd ever hoped for from running
every day, even when I don't
want to, is the feeling of having achieved
a small, unexpected virtue. To enter
the Forum that way, alone, surrounded
by the fragments of an ancient power, meant
that once again life was stranger
than I wanted it to be,
less expected, less achieved.

When the cry of a baby
comes floating down from above,
it is only demanding to be brought
from afar the love we all need,
and then to be held
until we sleep so that we may dream
of our overwhelmed lives, lives
that were never meant to be jogged,
only suckled, then held, then allowed
to grow up until they become
just too much. It's so good
to take a shower afterward,
after trying to pace myself
so that nothing will surprise me.
So good to collapse on a bed
in Rome and lie naked,
still wet in the new heat of a day
barely begun and already
too much. But I belong
to it now. I am strange enough,
having put on
the little red shorts and run out into it,
thinking I knew what I was doing.

SIX DAYS WITH FRA FILIPPO LIPPI'S FRESCOES IN THE DUOMO AT SPOLETO

1 *First Day: The Death of Mary*

The mother of God lies wrapped in a burnt-
orange sheet. She is outside, near
pines and moss, as if her bedroom
has become the whole world.
Away from which, at the end,
she turned her exhausted face.
There is something so unposed
about Mary's body, as if death
is a kind of afterthought:
oh, yes, then this happens.
Lippi has trusted us
with so many details, we who
are still alive. It's up to us
to love the world as it really is.

As I leave, a woman stands alone
in the back of the Duomo and prays, touching
her breast and forehead in the ritual way:
here I am again, God, putting the signs
of your suffering on my flesh.
She stares unwaveringly at the altar
and does not turn as I walk past.

2 Second Day: The Annunciation

Gabriel cannot look at Mary while he speaks.
Further back from his news
there are six plane trees thick with leaves.
Perhaps after he's gone
she can walk there. Perhaps
those green Umbrian cliffs
will console her for his news:
she must give birth to a child
who will grow, then suffer,
then die. She must become a mother.

3 Third Day: Mary's Death and the Face of God

God's memorized all the cues:
it's time to welcome Mary to heaven.
The white beard, the bovine calm.
Perfection seems to make him
sleepy. I keep looking down below
on the painted earth where an astonished
adolescent watches at Mary's bed:
he is pale with grief that she is gone.

Nearby, full-grown saints stand calmly.
They believe all is well. But the pale one
knows. He understands that when the mother goes,
part of life leaves with her,
never to be returned. I envy these saints,
the ones who wear gorgeous blue robes
and walk calmly through the world's
paintings. But it is the boy who guides me,
helps me peer, without turning away,
into the face of Mary's death.

4 *Fourth Day: Lippi in Heaven*

Forget God. Look at the daisies
in heaven. Look at the angel
with the hips. Forget God's droopy-
lidded peace. Don't miss that looped
smile of the angel on the left.

        Fra Filippo Lippi,
I read all about you today. They call you
the "dissolute priest": a jealous
husband shot you to death. In *your* heaven,
you just had to paint those robes
that are themselves a kind of flesh,
folds of a second skin
draped teasingly over the first. You must
have loved knowing that centuries later our eyes
would stray from God's dull face
to the hips of angels, their palms, and then those white
daisy petals so like lily pads slick
with water. All this flesh spread out
across heaven for us to look up to
as we raise our eyes in prayer
and see our world in paradise,
our heaven of cupped hands and earthly needs.

5 *Fifth Day: A Color with Which to Drape the Day*

Orange, orange, and again orange. Spread it
over her body, the mother
of God. She's dead now, so give it
some black, some faded blue,
give orange all the room it needs
to drape the world, this lovely tomb.
Break it slowly over the cow
in the manger. Let it stretch out
as skin. The smallest angel
over by the crib: let her be
lightly faded by its smeared
strangeness. And the baby's halo,
a circle of rust or dusty
sunlight, the exact shade that returns
each morning, first thing before
the sun rises, before the birth of God.

6 *Sixth Day: Love, the Manger*

It's not time to plod, to carry,
to pull, to work, to push, to be
milked. It's time to stand still, to adore.
Those animals that have learned to live
from human hands lean forward, their
gray eyes stricken with mild attention.

There's Mary looking down at her child,
there's Joseph looking up toward her.
Meanwhile, the cow concentrates
on the delicious weedy earth and the baby placed on earth.
Love is like this, the amazing
Lippi says: you concentrate and
concentrate, but still there is more to see.

AT FIFTY

1

It is a Sunday afternoon in Rome and the young policeman is so bored he studies his own fingernails as if they are a profound text with the most serious ramifications. At fifty, it makes sense that on your first day in Italy you come here with JoAnn, here where the little café spills out onto the street and the coffee is the best in all Rome, which is to say, in all the world.

It is heaven to arrive in Rome on a Sunday afternoon with a woman who knows how to read maps. The quiet unwinds in the square like a bolt of shimmering cloth.

At fifty, you get at least one Sunday afternoon in Rome so quiet that the voices of women speaking two streets away carry from stone to stone, like music bouncing off the walls of a cave, that music the Italians call a language. This is the only Sunday afternoon in the world, the first light and the last silence. At fifty, it makes sense that you surround yourself with stone, but warm stone, stone that is like the pulp of a fruit so ripe it has no choice but to fall to earth. You'd better order another coffee; you'd better sit here a long time trying to figure out how to find words for the way the buildings come together in this small square, meet at such odd and improbable angles, how they seem to collide, but in the friendliest possible way: like a father wrestling with his children, or a jigsaw puzzle constructed by a child who is putting a city together for the first time, laughing all the while, spending a few centuries at it as you would love to spend a few centuries trying to describe it. Though you'd better stop now, you'd really better lean across the small table covered with green cloth and kiss the woman you love.

Rome/For JoAnn

2

At the Campo dei Fiori, no one seems to mind that you sit on the base of a statue and watch as the vegetables and fruits are unloaded. At fifty, you keep an eye out for others who are also around fifty: the woman in the polka-dot blouse and high heels sorting lettuce; the man setting up shop from his VW bus; the other man in the beard and suspenders who slept all night in front of Pizzeria Virgilio. And straight above, in the slowly whitening sky, a quarter moon, which is also fifty years old. And fifteen or twenty swallows whose age you don't even bother to guess. A white-haired man in shorts sings as he carries a huge silver scale from a small car over to his mound of purple plums. You listen carefully to the ones who reach sixty and can't help singing. The man who slept on the sidewalk pulls a white cap out of his back pocket, puts it on and goes to work picking up trash from the sidewalk and putting it into the nearby bin. At fifty, you could do worse than sit with seven pigeons at dawn near the foot of an ugly statue. You could do worse than walk toward the long strip of sunlight at the far end of the square as two Filipina nuns in dove gray habits move past you, both of them smiling because it's dawn, and it's Rome, and they believe in the dear God of love whose true name is friendship.

Campo dei Fiori/Rome/For Deborah Keenan

3

It is time to lean. And you do just that, your upper back muscles against the cool marble of the Pantheon. Some call it the most perfect building in the world. Why would you ever disagree, the cool marble against your shoulder blades, the whole scooped-out feeling of the place and its comforting circular shape as you lean back and look up at the hole of light far above? There is something ghostly about this space, so gray and calm, so posed: as if it was created in order to bring into being a permanent dusk, a perfectly balanced twilight beyond the reach of time.

You sit down on the marble floor, put your back against the marble wall, and don't move a muscle, here where the shadows come to lay down their burden of light. It is such a pleasure to turn your back on the city and enter a building composed entirely of marble and soul, a place where no one lives, but anyone who wishes may enter, may stay as long as they want, may lean against marble until its darkness becomes their own, until its circular soul—unlit by anything but a nickel of sky—becomes their soul. You are beginning to learn how to look at light when it enters your life through one small eye so far away, it seems not to be part of your world at all. You may just stay here forever. Here with your marble and your soul, your permanent twilight where once upon a time the gods were worshipped, those dark ones who travel with the speed of whispers, called into being so that the shy, ungainly shapes of our longing might have a home.

Rome

4

You wake with a feeling of foreboding: something terrible will happen today. And then you remember: it's not what will happen, but what has happened. It was four years ago on this day that your father died. Four years ago that you sat with him, telling him—at long last—that you loved him, though he could no longer hear you.

Here is what you do: you sit at the window at the same time of day that he died and look at the stone wall. It is lined with flower pots, each one filled with geraniums. You sit and you look, and you let the work of beauty enter you, the effort it took to build the stone wall, the care someone puts into seeing that seventeen pots of geraniums thrive. Because that, too, is part of the confusing news that you are meant to receive: not only is there death in the world, but there is beauty. What is confusion anyway, except a mystery for which someone thinks there should be a solution?

On the dusty path outside your window, a small bird about the size of a sparrow. Its small black body is very still in the huge sunlight. There is nowhere else it needs to be other than where it is. You sit at the window and you watch the bird. You have an appointment to keep on the anniversary of your father's death, an appointment with your father, who today has come to you in the body of this small bird, bathing in the soft feathery dust of a hot summer's morning.

Spoleto/In memory of James Wallace Moore

5

It's the father of Saint Francis you feel yourself drawn to. Not the saint, but the father of the saint, a man in his fifties, according to Giotto, gray faced and clearly worried. His son, the saint-to-be, has just stripped to show how serious he is about his poverty. A church father has draped a towel around him, but clearly Francis would prefer to be naked. Giotto has painted him with his face turned upward—and who wouldn't look up if God's hand had just broken through the clouds like a descending airplane? Francis looks absolutely sure of himself in the way that only someone in their early twenties can pull off: his gaze is focused beyond this world. Which means he misses the worry and sadness in his father's face.

You can't possibly argue with what became of this Francis. But how much wiser the father's face is than Francis's; how filled it is with love and suffering. The father is being restrained by a friend. He wants to move into the arms of his son to embrace him, to try to convince him to return home.

But nothing he can say or do will matter in the slightest. Like the father of Francis, you encounter more and more of these moments: what you love you can't control. The one you loved seemed inextricably bound to you, then disappears.

Yes, it is the father you want as your friend. You've got enough of the would-be saint in you already, the perfect young man who thirsts only for more perfection. If you could, you would sit with the father on the day after all this happened. Together you would speak of destroyed hopes, of sons who would be perfect and the pain they must cause. Together you would be amazed at the ways the world has taken each of you by surprise. Maybe you would even shake your heads a little and laugh: "Can you believe he actually took off his clothes?" he might say to you. It seems that you both admire this young man. Who knows, one of you says to the other, what might become of him.

Assisi

6

Go into the kitchen for a fig. Return to the window. Eat the fig slowly. Even the skin of the fig. Eat so slowly you don't miss a thing. Stand near the rain and let your fingers grow sticky with the green and purple juices from a fruit that knows no purpose other than to ripen. When the sun shines, then go out into it. When the rain speaks, then stay at its side and listen well. And when the fig falls, do, by all means, eat it.

Spoleto

from

WRITING WITH TAGORE: HOMAGES AND VARIATIONS

(2003)

1

I thought it was over for me,
that I had come to the end
of what I could do.
I was ready for sweet obscurity.
But it seems that you are not yet done with me.

Just when I'd finished everything
I thought was left to me to say,
you came looking for me
in the name of one last wish:
that my heart break open
all over again,
as if for the first time ever.

———

Today you came looking for me
where I was sitting in the garden;

I was so busy reading about you
I forgot to look up as you passed by.

But there was this sweetness in the summer air
and the leaves moved easily in the wind,

like a music someone has played for many years
and as I listened I felt such longing.

———

There is a place where the river turns desolate,
disappearing among the tall grasses.
I saw you there, standing in the silence
that begins at the first sign of darkness.

You spoke quietly, as if reluctant to interrupt
such silence. "I'm here," you said, at long last,
"to dedicate a lamp to darkness,
to the emptiness that must go on forever."

I asked you then, as if I had a right,
"Why waste your light like this,
holding it against the edge of a sky
that will never be done with its darkness?

My house, too, is dark and I am lonely
for your light." You stood for a long moment
just looking at me, wondering if I could
begin to hear the words you were about to say.

"I have brought my light," you said, whispering,
so I was forced to lean forward to hear,
"to the largest darkness I could find."

I watched how it vanished, your little lamp,
into the black room of a loneliness beyond any need
for comfort, where one day, if you answer this prayer,
I may finally learn to go.

———

Sometimes when I get drunk
from the delight I take
inside the sound of my own voice,
I forget who I am
and call out to you, Friend:
as if I had any idea
who you really are.

———

It is time now to set out
in my little boat. And yet,
I keep waiting here on shore.

I can hear birds calling to me
from the other bank of the river.
But still, I refuse to leave.

On this shore, there is only what I already know:
longing and silence.

On the other shore: music.
But how can I abandon
the fear that gave me

the only words I have
with which to call out to you?

2

In this world, people love each other
by holding on.
But your love is different.
Inside those rooms where people must let go—
funeral homes, temples, train stations—
that's where your work gets done.

———

You know how to refuse and you do it well.
This refusal is your most difficult mercy

and it has entered my life through and through.
Whatever comes from me alone,

you refuse to accept.
Day by day, you are teaching me

how to become worthy of those things
not mine to offer:

the sky, these trees, this life
I like to call mine

but which exists beyond the net
of my desires and self-pity.

Living as it seems I must,
surrounded on all sides

by your refusals,
I begin to become worthy.

———

The great music of this world
is made only by the true masters.
They are with you day and night.
This would be paradise,
but it has nothing to do with me.

One day while I sat alone at the kitchen table
humming a nameless song to myself,
you heard me and for no reason I can see
came to stand at my back door and listen.

It seems that you love us, too,
the ones who keep forgetting who you are.
Truly, we should pay better attention.
And yet, you stand with us anyway
as we slice the bread, then set the table for one,
not knowing why it is we are no longer lonely.

———

It was your choice, not mine.
It was you who made me this way,
so that I can never come to the end of myself.
Such is your wish. Your joy
is that I am forever unfinished.
You love how I empty, then fill again
with you. You pocket me
like a flute. Sometimes at the top of a hill,
you take me out and put me to your lips.
When you breathe into me like that,
I am eternal and new.
At such times, my heart forgets
what a small thing it is.
Ages pass and still you pour me
out of your lips.
I have come to love my own emptiness:
without it, how could I be filled with you?

———

I make of my sorrow
a small gift for you.
It is so little to offer,
but if I were a beautiful dead one—
a star in your black sky—
I would give you, gladly,
my one shining death.
Wealth and fame are tokens
not mine to offer you.
But this sorrow that I offer
is absolute, no strings attached.
It is a grace beyond question,
and the only offering
I know you will not refuse.

———

Just a little strength is best,
so that I may bend lightly
under the weight
of my joys and sorrows.
Only enough not to ignore
the woman sleeping in the street,
the man who makes a morning
of going through the refuse.
Just a little strength, enough
to resist a greater strength gone bad.

———

Today, for no reason, there is this joy,
delicate as the eyelashes of a newborn.

And I feel it in the softness of the summer air,
how once again you are calling me

into the quiet secret of your presence.

3

The life that pulses under my wrist
as blood is the same life
that sways inside summer weeds.
This life that is mine day and night
also belongs to the world.
It is the same life
that rocks back and forth in the ocean,
that opens the gates at birth,
that closes the gates at death.

———

When the swallows
begin to disappear
as you wrap them in darkness.

Do for me
what you do for the earth
and the things of this earth:

cover me in darkness
and let me disappear
inside sleep's folded wing.

———

People take whatever meanings they want
from my words. Yet the real meaning

goes where the river goes,
as it passes through the fields

and small towns of this darkening world
you have shown me how to leave.

———

Even when my father died,
you were there, late that night,
as my mother and I sat on her small porch
listening to the ones who find their voices after dark,
crickets and night hawks.
I knew you were there
because I did not think to ask, "Mother,
what time is it now where he has gone?"

I see now by the light death casts,
and the barrier of time breaks up inside me.
What a strange joy it is, this new carelessness I feel—
things that I longed for, things that I got—
finally, I can let them go.
Who is there to say
that we have done too much or too little?
I will no longer need my coyness
or the sweet way I have of hiding in corners.
My work now is to crown death with life.

from

LIGHTNING AT DINNER

(2005)

YOU ARE HUMAN

But why not be this lake instead,
icy blue, and the little white curls
of waves, its absolute refusal
to be human? Why not be a thing?

Why not be a place
you'd go to get away
from your mother's frontal lobe "eroding"
as the faxed medical report has it?

Why not a lovely blue-turning-green
and why not the removal of all feeling?

Maybe she'd rather you be a lake,
a way to lie still in the world,
a melted-down pool of snow,
a place to rest.

You could let yourself wash up on foreign shores.
Or be the surface across which boats might ply their trade,
taking humans from the one shore in sun
to the other side in shade.

You remember humans, don't you?
The ones who row the boat,
who act for all the world
as if they know where they are going?

BRIEF LIVES

An anthology called *Brief Lives*. Not the writings of people who lived briefly, as I had thought. But rather the lives of the famous, written about briefly. It's hard not to admire them. They came, they conquered, they left the scene entirely. Their lives make a sort of graph: perfect.

And the rest of us? Nothing brief about them, these lives of ours: so-and-so was born. His grandmother befriended him. He hid in lilac bushes. He called Emma Jean Kendell a bad name. He was angry, then afraid. He loved badly, then well, then both at once. His father disappeared in his own time. A cardinal sang. He went to visit his dying mother, letting himself in with his own key. She is taking a shower. He listens to the water running from another room. It has taken them both forever—all their lives—to get to this point. There's no way to be brief, no way to get it over quickly.

GIVEN YOUR SPECIES

It's something else, the man says, when your daughter at thirteen sits up
    in bed and howls.
Not a nurse comes running: they're used to the sound pain makes inside
    her throat
and not a thing they can give to ease her unless it kills her.

He stands at the head of the bed. She won't have him
hold her hand since the pain only worsens. That's something else, he says,
that's suffering. You can see it one way,

he says, about snow, and call it beautiful, another and call it useful, a
    third way
might be *just stop it,* to beg it *stop falling.*

You might, given your species,
want to believe her suffering will end, even now, even while she is alive.
I can't believe it, he says,

how the snow keeps falling: of falling there is more, he says,

then more again. What it is, he says, we are meant to make of such a world,
I don't know, and if I did, I wouldn't say, not even to myself, let alone to you
who are my friends, each of you in your own way needing to believe

this is not your life, your daughter, not your species at all.

BRIEF LIVES: WARNING

6 A.M., the hour of the serious fishermen
who stand quietly in orange slickers
as they sway slightly in the small boats
far out to sea. Those ancient warnings,
the pelicans, patrol the world closer at hand.
It is the hour when the nurse tries to wake my mother,
then lets her fall back again
into the sea. Some fish are not worth
the trouble. *Asleep again, asleep again,*
her heart rejoices. And the great escape continues,
alone, in darkness, far under the surface.

WHEN I WAS A BOY I WAS

three gulls before the storm, far out
in the ocean. Their easiness, even though
something difficult is coming.
Surrounded by the vastness
of a life yet to be lived,
I floated in the large wind
of my childhood,
read my books on magic
and threw my ball again and again
into my mother's bed of lilies,
waiting patiently, the good boy I was,
for all that easiness to end.

POMPEII

At the motel, near where the dead
haven't moved in centuries,
there is a pool. A boy carries
a tall lily, as if it is a sacred lamp
the wind could blow out.
His mother sleeps by the pool's edge.
Mama, he calls out,
and louder, *Mama.*
This time she wakes.
The son gives his mother the lily,
then runs away, as if
afraid he will be caught
loving someone that much.
The lava is about to flow again
and the only way to stay alive
is to run fast his whole life long,
never stopping, never looking back
at the one face his life has given him
no choice but to love.

BRIEF LIVES: VACATION

See how everything is a secret?
his dying mother says to him in the dream.
She had taken the oil, greased her body
and was ready to swim far out,
all the way to the end.
So this is what they mean
by vacation, he thinks to himself,
awake now, looking at the sea.
So this is what they mean:
green, turquoise, silver, the ruin
and rise again of waves,
colors dying inside other colors.

LIGHTER NOW

My mother can name for you
the specific and complicated reasons
cheetahs sleep upstairs.
She can give you a keening
disguised as a polite whisper.
But if it's a little happiness
you want, try someone
a bit farther away
from death. The closer she gets,
the quieter it becomes
inside her head. As if she is listening
to the god over there in the corner,
the one hiding behind the cheetah
who can barely be heard.

I could have gone on loving her
forever, even in her old form,
when everything she said
made a kind of sense, when anger
and bitterness and forgiveness
never got enough
of throwing each other around.
But this is easier yet,
now that she is down to sighs
and those long unpunctuated silences
without beginning or end.

"I see,"
said my mother, without inflection,
after I told her how nice
the nursing home is where soon
she will be continuing,
uninterrupted,
her whispery disappearance
from this earth.

"I am trying to care about
what you are saying,"
she said to me today,
making the effort
to work it out, just exactly
who I am and why
it should matter to her
how much I love being here
in Italy. Cypresses,
I did not bother to say to her,
cypresses appear out of nowhere
just before dawn
to shepherd the night
back down its long aisle,
their needles still wet
with dew, damp and pleasing
to the touch.

I DON'T THINK WE NEED TO KNOW

I don't believe we need to know what below zero feels like.
Or why we die: that, too, I don't think we need to know.
Why life is hard? I think not.

It's hot inside, it's cold out:
that's already a lot to know. That love comes and goes,
that we grow old slowly and then suddenly not.

It helps to know that snow is a god fallen to earth.
Sometimes it helps to let in the world a bit:
some wind, a few flakes, the sound of ice cracking.

Stars, for reasons we'll never know, help show us
who on earth we are and how to bear it here and how
far away we are from knowing why we are small.

Who knows why we love or why we die,
or what exactly wonder is,
demanding that I touch it as if it were the beloved

and I the young bride, believing.

BRIEF LIVES: FORGIVE HIM

He simply did not see how the universe opening
inside him was the same as the river inside his mother
unwinding at its own pace, taking her away,
following the only course it knows. He did not see
that even the love he feels for her does not belong to him.
He is of the species that wants to believe in a separate self.
Forgive him this greed, this unending need
to make her life his own.

IT IS NOT THE FACT THAT I WILL DIE THAT I MIND,

but that no one will love as I did
the oak tree out my boyhood window,
the mother who set herself
so stubbornly against life,
the sister with her serious frown
and her wish for someone at her side,
the father with his dreamy gaze
and his left hand idly buried
in the fur of his dog.
And the dog herself,
that mournful look and huge appetite,
her need for absolute stillness
in the presence of a bird.
I know how each of them looks
when asleep. And I know how it feels
to fall asleep among them.
No one knows that but me,
no one knows how to love the way I do.

LIGHTNING AT DINNER

Basta! shouts the waiter,
then laughs each time the sky
is rent, delighted.
"Such a long journey,"
my failing mother said,
her voice calm and steady,
crossing seven time zones.

Light gone,
you and I sit in the dark. Our hands
touch, finally, hours
after our argument.
This sudden warmth, palm
to palm: as when thunder stops,
the suddenness of all that silence.
Or the aftershock—deafening—
when an only son
is given to understand
his mother's business with him
is completely done.

BLOOD HARMONY

1

If there is a god, then the god is not speaking,
only breathing in and out
through the mouth of my mother.
Her repeated rasps
and that small tuneless humming
are all this god has left of her
with which to work,
these and the thick gravel
of her cough, the sound of a gate
being forced:
won't quite close, won't quite open.

I sit in front of what the inevitable will do
to any one of us, how it takes us away
breath by breath.
Listen,
you, God, or whatever
you call yourself now
inside her, pulling her breath in and out:
she was once my mother.

The shy nurse knocks, comes in,
"Is there anything I can get you?"
I say, "No," and she, too, shakes her head,
of course there is nothing to get you.
She closes the door behind her
as she leaves us to our work.
It is not beautiful, this dying,
but it is what this god has for a tool.
And the moon sets
on the last night
God will ever use her
as a way to breathe.

———

Mother, I address you now as a victor
speaks to the defeated:
there is a boat hidden down in the harbor.
It has no oars, no motor,
no need of a captain.
It is time now to escape the burning city,
torched beyond recognition.
Let the tide carry you out to sea.
Don't try anything as hopeless
as being. I tell you this as the one
who has spent his life
trying to force happiness on you.
No one will come to your rescue.
Only sky and water now.
Only horizon.

Outside your window, the lake and the setting moon,
trapped inside the smoke pluming up from the factory,
turning it as gray as your own sinking face,
this day that will take you with it
as it leaves.

2

Afterward,
they covered with a simple sheet
the face that had once been
yours and now seemed empty
of the god no longer inside it,
no one ordering you
to continue the cruel, miraculous work
of being.

Almost immediately we left that place
where for two years you had been turned,
one side to the other each day,
like an animal roasting, slowly being prepared.

Meanwhile, your grimace still in place,
you lay alone under fluorescent lights
in a room no one ever visits alive
unless they are paid to do so.
Sometime during that long night,
maybe while we ate, maybe later,
while we were washing dishes,
a stranger took away your sheet
to be washed, ironed, and folded.
Then quickly, without ceremony,
you were given to the flames.

   3

There is no turning back,
no way to flee to another country.
Gray is the new national anthem:
what matters now is not what you say,
but to whom you pledge allegiance.
What matters is: do you see her sycamore?
Her cardinals? The moon she swore surprised her
each time?

4

At twelve, I decided I should become a saint.
And now, surely the time has come
to put on brown robes, the rough sandals
only those holier than us
strap to their feet.
Time to look out from the sad, crazed eyes
of grief's holy confusion
onto the cut glass of February sunlight.
And time at long last for the unfamiliar, intriguing scent of self-forgetfulness,
the scent of the earth as it is.

Time to pray to the world as a saint might pray:
once you were my mother, once I was yours.

—————

The world is beautiful, yet fails its beauty.
What choice, but to love the failings themselves
as she loved the clouds out her hospital window,
mistaking them for birds,
never quite able to remember
their names.
I could hear her tuneless humming
as if, blood harmony, it were also being hummed
inside me, and I saw what my mother saw,
those rain-filled shapes she mistook
for robins, seagulls, sparrows.
Not a god myself,
still I see how it works in heaven:
Birds, she said.

LEARNING A NEW LANGUAGE

(Colorado Springs, Colorado)

Last night you sat on the couch
conjugating verbs. I was at the window,
one eye on the dark and untranslatable
stone of the mountain. But the other eye
watched you as you chanted Italian.
I too am learning a verb: to love—
past, present, imperfect, future.
But I keep forgetting how hard it is
to speak a language so foreign
to my tongue. Later,
in bed, you are still reading
from the book of answers.
I fall asleep with the light on,
my back fitting easily into the small cave
of your warmth. I dream you learned
the imperfect, then whispered it
in my ear. The next morning
I wake up first and sit
before the same window.
The world's imperfect beauty
sings its song into my ear.
Out of the darkness,
the mountain rises into light,
untranslatable joy,
happiness in the present tense.

8:03 P.M.

The spread quilt of a humid summer in Umbria.

If there is life after death, it is this.

And she is naked on the bed behind me.

The swallows dipping, then rising again,
refusing to let the sun set all by itself.

Even the whine and rasp of motorcycles.

Even this strange tiredness.

Don't you know where you are?

The pasta is boiling in paradise.

The one dirt road
leads everywhere I need to go.

A naked woman gets up off the bed
and asks, "When do you want to eat dinner?"

The only answer to every question in paradise is

now.

IT IS THE HOUR

A small park in Ravenna, a pocket of shade darkening
behind the statue of the general. It is the hour
of tuneless whistling, of serious naps,
of frowning men sitting under pine trees
with thick books, of the girl in her wheelchair,
moaning. It is the hour when you remember the greed
behind your impatience, and the pain it caused,
the hour of remorse, of marigolds
shining their deep yellows and oranges.

RED POPPY, ALMOST DARK UNDER AN OLIVE TREE

It's only beauty
and of a kind too obvious even to name.
And yet, when you touch me in that way you have,
absentmindedly driving me crazy,
only the red poppy under the olive tree will do,
only stars given chase by sunrise.

POINTLESS

I don't think swallows were meant to become
emblems of the beloved, absolute capitals
in the alphabet of happiness.

And yet, with swallows
there is no arguing
when it is 3 P.M. by cathedral bells,

though nothing will come
of this happiness,

pointless as the soft ears
of the rabbit carried carefully in its cage
by the woman in dirty blue jeans,

lips downturned, sorrowful and erotic,
as she slept next to her beloved rabbit

on the slow train from Rome to Spoleto, the train
that leaves in the heat of noon, the one no one ever takes.
But we did, you and I, plus two labial rabbit ears

and the anointed lips of a sleeping beauty I will say
is part of my life. Now is not the time to unpack; no, now is the time to love,

as the bells go drifting down,
all the way down to 4 P.M. and counting, they cannot
help themselves.

TEACHING THE DOG NOT TO NIP

Do you think it's easy,
not biting
the one you love?
Try loving someone so much
your mouth is only at home
in the place where your teeth
meet the flesh
of your beloved. Try
not tasting the flesh,
not taking in your mouth
the beloved, not
going all the way.

WHAT TO WRITE WHEN A LANDSCAPE
IS TOO BEAUTIFUL

You do not need to say red poppies,
or even, silver light after rain.
God forgive me all pettiness:
olive trees, olive trees, olive trees.

AT NIGHT WE READ ALOUD *THE AENEID*

But slowly. At this rate,
Rome may never get built.
Each night, the boat of our voices
carries us toward our dreams
on the dissolving tide of a world
both strange and bloody. A world
in which love does not matter,
though our love makes of it
a place we can bear to live.

ON THE TRAIN TO VENICE

The first and least important mistake
was to take the train on Sunday, September 1st,
the last day of vacation for millions of Italians.
Though the train was packed,
we had thought to bring sandwiches.
We ate while everyone around us—sitting, standing,
filling every possible inch of floor space—
went profoundly silent and watched
as if we were demonstrating a new technique
for brain surgery, one never tried before,
gone horribly wrong.

Not long after we finished, out of nowhere
came sandwiches, water, and fruit,
every last bit of it offered all around,
especially to those who had brought
nothing with them. Such kindness
and pleasure, such gratitude, except
on the part of the two Americans
who had eaten their fill alone,
in silence, as if the world was empty
of everything but themselves.

AGAINST EMPIRE

Small olives taste best.
Small stars shine farthest.
Small birds call
most sweetly. Small lives,
we are small, small lives.

SOON

It's really over now, summer, I feel
the next thing in the heaviness
of the grapes as they stagger downward
toward the ripeness
they were born for.
Someone with more power than us
can't take his mind off war.
No one ever told him the truth,
how bewildered he looks, how sad,
and how desperately he seems to long
for danger. Meanwhile, light surrenders
by 6:30 P.M. and rusty barbed-wire fences reappear
where once summer grass covered them
as an ocean covers a treasure sunk long ago.

Not an ounce left of that summer heat that wants of us
only the pleasure of our shirtless company,
no more red poppies like little fragile gods
that have dedicated themselves to ditches
and other lost places where gods
so rarely appear. Yes, the gods have shriveled up
and though the man who sells ice cream in the mercato
still stands behind his chocolate, his lime,
his luscious vanilla and hopes for the best,
in his heart he knows.

Soon the man with the power will point his finger
and husbands will be ordered to put on their uniforms.
Soon, tears and bent heads, fields with the look
of raw wounds, raw wounds with the look
of abandoned fields.

It is the season when olive trees bend heavily
in the cold wind, scraping the ground
as if inviting earth to touch them.
Is it too late for that now? Too late
for one living creature
to touch another? The grandmother
holding the baby by the fountain has no choice
but to remember how happy
it is possible to be. The street cleaner
has the thoughtful brooding look
of a philosopher whose work has been unjustly ignored
for years. He drags his broom behind him
past the drugstore, past the newspaper stand,
past the shadowy boxes loaded down
with oranges from Morocco, cherries from Bari,
walks slowly back and forth across the square
refusing to clean what will only get dirty again.

9/9/02

WHAT IT'S LIKE HERE

It was nothing unusual. Just a woman, bare-knuckled
on a cold day, pushing an empty grocery cart up University toward hell.
You see it all the time on this planet of theirs.
I had been to what they call a movie. And I was what they call
happy. As you know, fate has given me a wife, beloved to me.
Yes, beloved is a thing they understand. Right now she is playing *come*
with the dog while I write this report. Sometimes she says to me,
"You are really from another planet!" I just hold my tongue.

There is hell around every corner here. There are people who are paid well
to ruin the lives of others. There are people strapped down
to chairs, then a button is pushed. Smoke rises sometimes
off their bodies before they die. I do not tell you this
to shock you, but because you need to know there are planets
where such things happen. Even so, there is happiness
of a kind you would recognize. Right now there is snow,
a thing that divides itself up into many pieces,
then falls from the sky until all ugliness is covered.
"Beautiful day, isn't it," people say and it's not a question.

My question is, "Where do I go from here? What do you want of me?
Why was I born on this planet?" You'll want to know, did I stop
and help the lady. I did not. And you'll want to know
what does "beloved" mean, if not that. I don't know. I only breathe
one breath at a time. Not like you who breathe so many lives
at once. We drove home, my beloved and I. The movie?
It was called *Men of Honor*, a kind of dream
of how things should be. We didn't like it.
Nothing about it rang true. But we held hands anyway,
then went out into the bare-knuckled cold, described above.

CHRIST RESURRECTED

The miracle is not that he came back,
but that he was willing
to leave behind such stillness,
and so recently achieved.

SELF-PORTRAIT DOING T'AI CHI
IN CHINATOWN, 7 A.M.

                              Slowly
I turn my hips, as if
sex is my true country
and the poise of it
spreads evenly everywhere
blood flows.
                          Everything
must be done just so,
as in a dream when one ascends,
                        then flies,
leaving it all behind.
And the Lower East Side
reveals itself, from above, as a river
of lives unwinding towards the sea
into which, one day,
all of us will have slipped
                        quite easily.

                        There is a statue
they call Liberty. Countrymen,
it is a beautiful idea,
a woman rising from the water
bearing light.

                        Such thoughts
I think inside the slow hula
my body makes
                        of its need

to be silent,

                                         to move

with such fluid precision,

                                         to know

what it means to be of this world,

                                     while flying

ever so slowly toward the next.

IT

We are not it, but it requires us.
It does not accept this century or the last. It hasn't the taste
for starvation or gas. It is not a rooster,
but it loves the way the rooster needs everyone to know:
this day is made for roosters: do not lose all hope.

LAST NIGHT AT DINNER

for David Goldes

Someone is back with us,
someone who almost died.
I'm the bald one. I smile
and pass him the noodles. Can anyone
ever see all the way inside us?
Someone sits at eye level
across the table from me.
Our fathers died,
each in their own time.

An orange light hovers
over the clouded city,
though it's dark
and has been for hours.
As if somewhere a fire rages
out of control,
and we are its kindling.

The fish we eat is firm
and sweet. The son
of my friend charges a quarter
for his father to enter his room:
a bargain!
There is a secret life inside us
that knows the cost,
that is willing to pay the price.

WHEN THE DOG IS SICK

She eats white rice,
white rice only.
Little Buddha with your curved smile
of a tail, tell me
what life is like
for those who love
without condition or restraint.

GET USED TO IT, BEING

The day after the Day of the Dead
where do you put the bones
you don't need, the paint, the wig, the circles
in black around the eyes, the dead-white flesh?

I don't mind the dead,
when they are not yet fully grown,

knocking politely at the door. They want
a little sweetness, arriving costumed
in the skirt of not-being, wearing the smeared cape
that drapes what is and reveals what is not.

Trick or treat! Give or be soaped!
In greed and fear, in death's near light,
in need: get used to it, being.

The dead stand at the door and hold out their bowls,
little monks begging for more life;
and this one night we do not turn away
from how the dead need us to come to the door

and smile. We say, good costume, we say,
what can we give you from our still warm hands?

IT IS HARD NOT TO LOVE THE WORLD,

but possible. When I am like this,
even the swallows are not God.
Even the yellow school bus.
Even the children inside,
wanting out, are not God.

HAPPINESS

Uncle Vanya was sad last night, so bitter, bewildered and trapped, just like every other time I've seen him. "In two hundred years," he said, "perhaps they will have discovered how to be happy." Well, it didn't take that long. We know now that happiness is sitting in darkened theaters and watching failed worlds beautifully acted: the love affairs that turn ridiculous and the drunken impoverished dreams, the wistful hopes, and the fleeting moments of grace.

What happiness to go back again to the staged rainy night, the lightning, the sound of the revolver. Back to the dark and passionate purposes of love, the birch forest, the relief of experiencing a dreariness suffered through by someone else, then left when we walk out, after the play is finished, into the cold fall air. What happiness to know that all our mistakes have been made before, have been made over and over on one stage or another for at least one hundred twenty-five years. And then, too, the small moments of tenderness: whether acknowledged or not on stage, we in the audience saw them. Those dear familiar bald heads of the men, the hair turning white on the women. And the same pointless jokes, and the hearts, the same broken hearts. All that love and all that loneliness. Let the thunder begin, let the curtain rise.

CRICKETS WELL BEGUN

Here come those swallows yet again,
50s jazz from the terrace up above,
curl of cigarette smoke a table away
where the young man with the earring
holds forth to the young man with the earring,
crickets well begun, figs
at lunch, the boredom
now that there is nothing
not to love, quiet darkness coming,
Remembrance of Things Past
waiting on the cardboard box,
the mountains holding their blues
against the sky, the years going faster now,
and now tiredness like the hand of a lost brother,
heavy on my shoulder, so sure of its rights,
he's long overdue, the absent one, now come home at last.

LATE/LATER/LATEST

If I stood like this each evening near nightfall,
stood silent in June next to this olive tree,
if I could breathe in time to its breathing,
to the in of fading light, the out of oncoming darkness,
what fear could death then hold for me?

STRANGE WORLD

In the life before this one,
these evergreens
draped
with a thickly needled hush,
these bearers of fragrant shadows
smelling faintly of another world
as babies do after their bath—
in the life before this one,
these trees were hermits
who prayed steadily
through the long nights of self-hatred
and the even longer days
filled with wearisome unending fear.

Because of their stubborn devotion
to the invisible god
in which they believed
despite all lack of evidence,
they were allowed to come back
rooted in the deep earth of humility,
this time unafraid of the darkness
or the light.

Now they no longer need
to pray with words:
their whole bodies rise up
in thick-barked praise,
in needles shaking with delight,
even as they sink down
into secret black rivers
of roots
which circle the earth

in a slow measured flowing
unbothered
by the great triumphs
that occur on earth,
or the even greater failures.

We are not such marvelous hermits
and never will be.
These trees are from god.
And if it turns out there is no god,
still they have found a way
to come from him.
Strange and pitiable world—
it is still possible
for us to walk by an evergreen
and not bow our heads in prayer
as we would bow our heads
before any god
suddenly put in our path,
any god
singing of heaven and earth,
of darkness and light,
of the world to come
and the world that has always been.

AT LEAST

Since it seems the consensus that one day I must die,
seems all my friends, too, will go,
at least let there be thunder on that day.
And the steady comfort of a summer rain.
Since sound, they say, is the last thing to fail.

Let it be so. But if it cannot be,
if the season is bare of leaves, the death painful
and greed for the world still fiercely with us,
then let someone else be allowed our place on the white couch,
rain falling, the final sounds of a life listened to
and, without fear, let go of: listened to and let go of.

ON THAT DAY

Perhaps on the day time leaves me behind
like an earring
slipped behind a couch,
perhaps on that day: calm and humility.
But probably not. Probably, mostly fear.
Probably a long summer dusk,
swallows followed by bats.
If I'm lucky, an extra quilt
to throw over me at the last moment
because the nights are chilly here
and it is good to sleep the night through without waking.

WHAT DO I LOOK LIKE?

Clusters of dandelion seeds,

spent and beautiful,
casting themselves without worry or fear
into the very current of air that carries them away from themselves.

I have taken a shape
that loses itself in the wind, a common weed, without parent or child.
Everywhere I land, I feather again,
again begin without regard to beauty.

What do I look like?

This lilac-scented, windblown, gauzy, cardinal-throated spring.
No one need bother tell me ever again
what's up ahead.

As the purple lilacs feel, swollen and full, asway on their bent stems,
so I feel when someone picks me in huge handfuls,
puts me in water and keeps me for as long as I last.

from

INVISIBLE STRINGS

(2011)

Nowhere is there place
to stop and live, so only
everywhere will do:
each and every grass-made hut soon leaves
its place within this withering world.
                              Saigyō

LOVE IN THE RUINS

1

I remember my mother toward the end,

folding the tablecloth after dinner
            so carefully,
as if it were the flag
            of a country that no longer existed,
but once had ruled the world.

2

7 A.M. and the barefoot man

leaves his lover's house
            to go back to his basement room
across the alley. I nod hello,
            continuing to pick
the first small daffodils
            which just yesterday began to bloom.

3

Helicopter flies overhead

reminding me of that old war
            where one friend lost his life,
one his mind,
            and one came back happy
to be missing only an unnecessary finger.

4

    I vow to write five poems today,

look down and see a crow
      rising into thick snow on 5th Avenue
as if pulled up by invisible strings,
      and already
there is only one to go.

5

    Survived

another winter: my black stocking cap,
      my mismatched gloves,
my suspicious, chilly heart.

EPITAPH

He stole forsythia.
He lived for love.
He never got caught.

ALMOST SIXTY

1

No, I don't know

the way to get there.
Two empty suitcases sit in the corner,
if that's any kind of clue.

2

This spring night,

everyone at the party
younger than me
except for one man.
We give each other the secret password.

3

Tears? Of course, but also the marsh grass

near the Mississippi:
your whispers and mine,
and the dog's long contented sighs.

ON THIS CLOUDY MAY DAY

I keep thinking
maybe June is what I need
to make me happy.

THOSE OTHERS

We lived at the end of an empire.

Sometimes we gathered in huge auditoriums
    and tried to understand.
Our shame did not save us,
    nor our sadness redeem us,
as we came to understand
    how others, far into the future,
would look back at us,
    shaking their heads: we hoped
in sorrow; more likely, anger.

FIVE CHARMS IN PRAISE OF BEWILDERMENT

1

At first when you leave town,

the dog and I maintain dignified silence.
        After no more than two hours
I'm talking to her, after three
        she's telling me the story of her life.
I nod my head at every word,
        encouraging her
to take all the time she needs.

2

I have the vice

of courting poems.
        Pathetic, I know.
I also like to watch *Oprah*
        if no one is around to notice.
That's right,
        I court poems, I watch *Oprah,*
I even let out wordless sighs late at night,
        and call them
my spring fields ploughed, my ready earth.

3

Sitting quietly at dusk, I'll admit

my life goes like this:
        dark branches
scratching the still darker window.

4

   "How are you?"

I ask a woman at work.
        "I have no idea,"
she replies,
        sounding pleased with herself
at the heartfeltness
        of her own bewilderment.

5

   We don't know,

can't possibly know,
        never have known,
never will know.
        We just don't know.

HOW WE GOT USED

The lousy passport photos were a start:

followed by the business
          with the coffee machine going whoosh whoosh,
then nothing.
          Your mother died, followed by mine.
After that,
          just attention to detail, plus touch.

THE TEMPEST: ACT 2 (SCENE 2 ENDS)

After "lead the way,"

the stage door opens onto coolness.
    Actors stand outside
between scenes, smoking.
    Their faces are bruised with makeup
like plums newly ripened on a tree,
    the true sweetness showing through.

BIRTHDAY

1

Almost sixty:

from now on
        even begonias are amazing.

2

As in a dream

in which a light flashes
        and one has no choice
but to follow it,
        I ran after
the lightning bug
        along the railroad tracks
the night before my sixtieth birthday,
        a little drunk, unafraid,
laughing my fucking head off.

3

Only in dreams now

does my mother tell me
        to remember my sweater
on these cool summer evenings.

4

Walking past my two favorite pines,

still dripping from the rain,
    I point them out to you,
and you smile,
    and I am still sixty.

5

Cottonwoods in wind:

shakiness
    is the only way.

FIRST THE GOOD NEWS:

the girls still wrap blue scarves
      around their long necks,
then step out into the December air,
      laughing.

ALL THAT TALK OF THE MOON

1

When the woman across the way cries out at night

while making love,
      it is like the flash of lightning
that reawakens for a moment
      the ash
of all the fires
      that have previously burned us to the ground.

2

I love so badly

it amazes me
      you put the peony in my room.

3

Sometimes regret is simply all there is,

Saigyō
      and all your talk of the moon
is only so much talk of the moon.

IN THE LONG AFTERWARD

Almost 8 A.M., curtain drawn shut, lying in bed naked:

it's not the same as sex,
        but close
as a door slams,
        a shoe crunches on gravel,
walking away.
        Then the long afterward of lying still—
happy, lonely,
        who can say which—
the world
        just as it is, and the lover too,
just so.

WAITING TO TAKE OFF

I try not to listen to the directions
       to the emergency exits,
how close they are,
       how very well lit.

AFTER DINNER

For many years, unable to speak the language,

I have sat silently at tables with Italians.
     Tonight, too. But this time I don't mind.
Joy enters the voices. Then sadness.
     We sit in moonlight, drink wine
until I understand every last word.

     After dinner, you and I do the walk
around the old fortress where power
     had once seemed the point of things.
The sound of crickets and a samba band, faintly,
     from the Communist Party
party, far down the hill. Our dog
     seems to lead the way, but really,
everything leads everything else
     around the abandoned fortress.

MIDNIGHT AND THE LOW SOUND OF WATER

from a stone fountain. His dog suddenly barking at us,
  an old man, vocal chords gone,
puts his hand to his throat, whispers through his voice box,
  Tomorrow
he will be your friend for life.

THREE DAYS IN SPOLETO

1 *(Tuesday)*

Some days, I am capable

only of caring about my new chestnut-colored shoes
    with the red laces, which in Italy
seem demure, but in Minnesota
    will give off the faint whiff
of a clown gone overboard, drowning
    in his own ridiculous sea.

2 *(Friday)*

The young Americans arrive,

backpacks and loud voices,
    such excitement
at being Elsewhere. "I miss my mother,"
    I hear one say to another,
standing at a railing from which you can see
    darkness coming from miles away
across the valley, the same darkness
    you will be given to call your own
after your own mother is gone.

3 *(Saturday)*

In the café yesterday,

the one that looks out on the ruins
    of the old amphitheater,
I was in the middle of reading
    yet another poem about death
when I looked up. A man was standing there
    hand open, silently hoping
I might give.

He stared straight at me,
the brown skin of his palm like a blind eye
        looking out at nothing.
I shook my head no
        and went back to my book, death
returning to death.

BLOOD IN OUR HEADLIGHTS, CAR WRECKED, THE BOAR DEAD

Out of the darkness, men come
        with knives. They work quickly,
muttering back and forth.
        By the time the police arrive,
the boar is gone. The foreigners,
        each one of us, stand around
the wrecked car,
        everyone still alive.

        And then

the moment becomes a story,
        cut open as completely as the boar had been,
all of us making use of it
        in whatever ways we need
until our lives and the names
        we were given never to let go of,
go.
        And even laughter and even our fears:
gone,
        along with the boar and our bewilderment,
traceless now inside the unending sound
        of crickets, the brown dust
soaked in blood.

SLEEPING WITH *MONA LISA*

The young woman on the train

uses as a bookmark
    a postcard of the *Mona Lisa*.
She sleeps while in the distant field
    at the edge of the painting
just poking up through her book
    I see the light da Vinci loved,
the blue light of ambulances at night
    when they pulse out their warnings.

TRIUMPHS

The triumphs in his life
were so quiet, he should be ashamed.
        That she would touch his back
on the correct place
        at dawn.
That when it came to swallows
        near dusk he acknowledged
no peer.
        Happiness was never a thing
he could claim as a specialty.
        But sitting by the window
in the middle of an endless winter night,
        now that is a thing
he can do. Decorum
        under a black sky, patience
in moonlight, dozing, then waking again.
        That the sight of the dog sleeping mattered
was a triumph
        not just anyone
could understand. Or the thought
        of sleep itself and its rose
pillowcase, or leaving it behind
        at 4 A.M., sitting
at that dark window,
        wide awake for no reason,
letting himself get distracted again
        by the ruined garden
where the neighbor lives
        who rarely bothers to speak
now that her son has died.
        She likes to stand by her wrinkled poppies
early in the morning,
        when she thinks she is alone.

But she is not alone. *Triumph*
     was always the wrong word,
wasn't it? No,
     not triumph; but something much closer,
like the remaining leaves on October trees,
     all glory and dissolution.

TRYING TO LEAVE SAINT PAUL

1

Little streets of Saint Paul

that lead nowhere. One of them
      ends where quiet drunks sit
in the old September grass
      on top of a hill.
Streetcars used to run here,
      through a tunnel cut into the hill.
The sun rides so low
      in the cloud-filled western sky,
it makes the empty bottles glow.

2

How far away

it is possible to go from Saint Paul
      in a single night of raucous dreams:
I wake up before dawn,
      joyful, moon sliding in
through the slats
      of our broken bamboo curtain.

3

A boy and his father

cross the street. The first depends
      on the second. The second
fumbles for a map.

4

     Yesterday we almost did it,

took off from Saint Paul,
     driving south thirty hours
to Florida, almost gave in
     to sunlight, warmth, the sea.
The biopsy report had come back negative,
     making me greedy for more:
coconuts, fresh shrimp, crickets
     past midnight under a full moon.
I did so want
     to begin driving
and never stop.

THE FOUR STAGES OF LOVE

1

My father: how he lifted

his glass at our wedding,
      and with shaking hand
welcomed love into my life.

2

Getting out of bed,

you run the bath water
      and I sleep a moment longer,
dreaming of a Greek island
      and flowers in a deep cavern.
Very slowly I climb down
      for a closer look.

3

Driving the December road to Saint Paul

in winter sunlight,
      Bill Evans on the radio. Maybe
this is actually paradise,
      you said, and on we went
from there.

4

I want to believe it

when the pine tree out my window
      tells me I don't have to be afraid
for my own death, not even,
      Love, for yours.

ABOVE ALL, DON'T FORGET

that empty lacrosse field at dawn,
    the brown grass of December,
the solitary runner jogging past
    under the three pine trees
you see each morning first thing,
    even before you remember
to worry about what you do deserve,
    what you don't.

INSTEAD OF CALM

1

An old man reads the newspaper

with complete focus, such a peaceful face,
    and that checked, immaculate cap.
Slowly his fingers move down each column,
    line by line.
Nothing is missed, not one single scandal
    or horrific accident.
God forbid I ever become so calm.
    Head bowed, he sees it all,
never smiling or frowning.

2

After your cousin's death—

sudden, accidental at eighteen—your father
    told me you went for a long run
along the edge of a golf course, then around
    a small pond. You ended
coming up the hill to your house
    at the very place you began.
You were still breathing deeply,
    regularly, and there was nothing
to be done for it.

OF ALL PLACES

1

After the death

of our young friend's brother,
    she looks at me differently,
almost with suspicion,
    as if there was something about this life
I had deliberately not told her.

2

That all calm is a false calm

I keep learning again and again.
    And yet,
the sound of water falling on stone
    early one warm June morning,
in this world of all places.

3

Her friends come now

every day since the death of her brother
    to walk the floor along with her
as she sweeps up
    in the little café
where we came to know her
    before the grief of her true life began.

POEM WITHOUT AN ENDING

Listening to acorns fall
such a lovely sound
I thought it was the whole poem
until I saw the girl in the paper
with the mussed hair
the bombed bus
no one bothering yet
to close those two black eyes

MOONLIGHT SHINING BARELY

1

When the drunk woman approached us

wanting only one dollar—something to do with Lent
        and a flat tire—
we gave it to her. It was a cold February night,
        raining. Afterward, she put the cross
across her own forehead with her own fingers
        as if she were both priest and penitent,
and we were the rest of the congregation,
        waiting patiently in line
both to forgive and be forgiven.

2

One car moving slowly

at 5 A.M. on a dirt road
        across the river and then, suddenly,
this whole life is gone.

3

The more I study it now,

the art of my superiors, the more
        I see how it is mostly darkness.
Though sometimes at the edge
        of a canvas
a bit of moonlight shines barely
        on women mourning
a dead Christ, their faces ravaged
        by a kindness
unknown to me.

HER JOY

      She lines up a chair at her window,

sets a book next to the chair:
      everything waits for everything else
to catch up. At ninety,
      reading Proust in French,
still looking out the window.
      It all matters:
the postman with the well-trimmed beard
      who lives across the street,
his regular route;
      how each night
the sun sets and still the world goes on,
      even into darkness.

HOMEFRONT

1

Here at home

nothing changes. Middle-aged men
        send young men to war.
Old men wake up before dawn
        waiting for the light to come
as they gaze from a window
        at oak trees
arriving without haste out of the darkness,
        tears in our eyes,
not that they help.

2

"Maybe I should go to the Civil War cemetery and write a poem,"

I say. "Sounds like a really bad poem," you say.
        I sit in the lobby of the Hampton Inn instead
and watch TV images from Thailand,
        where the living hang on to palm trees
just above the raging flood
                for as long as they can.

IN THE SHADOW OF THE ROD AND REEL CLUB

1

Chilly morning at the sea: I see

jade-green water, the turquoise blue, eternity
        everywhere I look. But what really gets me
is the shape of your skirt on a hanger,
        hooked on the showerhead.

2

A single pelican flies by

with the feel about it
        of an ancient culture.
No one speaks that language anymore.

3

At the town harbor for the last time,

no doubt I will forget
        the way the black dog
on the wet sand chases the red ball
        until the end of time.

4

On the same day

the bomb goes off in Baghdad,
        I watch a green palm tree
climb easily into gray sky,
        rain whispering all down
its knotty, stubborn spine.

A wedding party dies.
The parents and the bride,
        the photographer
hidden in the wings,
        and the children
not yet conceived, also
        hidden in the wings.

    5

        Sitting by the sea, waiting for darkness:

after all, I've come this far.

    6

        Too bad. It's time to go,

but the fishermen will stay behind,
        working the shadows
in back of the Rod and Reel Club:
        steady now; be patient; just a little longer.

THANKSGIVING

1

The wet wood costs us real money,

but these dry chips he threw in for free.
      It's no way to run a business,
but our fire burns beautifully.

2

On Thanksgiving, the phone

suddenly stops working. For this, too,
      Lord, we give thanks.

3

Giant pines in November sunlight:

sitting inside their shadows
      what is death to me?

4

Everyone is always younger than me

and more beautiful. Actually,
      this arrangement works.

5

Three black dogs in gray light

at dusk, tails up, faces together:
      nothing is missing.

IF I COULD HAVE BEEN A BUDDHIST,

I would have accepted humbly,
     without judgment, the world
as it was given:
     the whisper
of my sister's voice on the phone,
     telling me of her friend's murder.

Instead,
     I love what I can:
your black hair on the white pillow,
     the sound of a crow calling out,
even as it grows more distant.

NEBRASKA FRAGMENTS

1

The unmoving shadows

of black-and-white cows,
       a river's blue vein.
Then sunlight
       flooding down on the confused hearts of those
going east on 80, those going west.

2

How many more years

will it go like this:
       cheap motel room outside Omaha,
a glimpse of the yellow ball
       under a desk,
the dog just too sleepy to fool with it?

DISAPPEARING IN AMERICA

1

At a coffee stand

in front of a World War I memorial
        near the school where I teach,
a young woman
        dispenses the sweet with the bitter.
People line up
        to pay her for it.

2

Will this be the day

when I stop
        on the way home from work,
even for a moment,
        at Hennepin and Lake
and bow my head?
        Do you know
the corner I mean,
        where they planted that little elm
which never quite took root?

3

It is difficult to call my own,

but impossible not to,
        this world
in which a boy,
        both legs shattered by a land mine,
then flown to New York,
        smiles from his bed
at the doctor who amputated them
        cleanly, just above the knees.

4

      My single star is gone, the one

I like to call mine. Instead, a thick haze
      of moonlight. Just as my mother did
when she was growing old, I sit in the darkness,
      getting used to how little I can see.

LAST NIGHT I DREAMED THAT MAN, THE ONE

from the photos on a leash.
     His slight moan
has nothing to do with sex, his fear
     is not a thing I know
what to do with, and yet,
     here we are in the same dream,
each of us ashamed
     that the other exists.

WHEN ALL ELSE FAILS

1

You make me laugh,

then I make you laugh, and so
      it goes, this last day of fall.

2

Those two, newly in love,

standing in a bookstore
      near the back:
for them, holding the same book,
      while helping each other
turn its pages,
      is enough.

3

The setting moon and the night

move silently in opposite directions,
      old friends
no longer needing to bother with words.

4

Last fall crickets: impossible

not to write
      one more poem.

THERE GOES THAT LITTLE MUTT FROM DOWN THE STREET

and the man, his owner,
        walking together in the cold
December darkness:
        love takes you
where you need to go,
        no exceptions.

ANNIVERSARY

1

      Reading the poet on Nothingness,

I suppose it is a higher calling than love.
      And yet, love
is what I have been given,
      not Nothingness.
Who am I to argue
      with the lesser fate:
twenty-five years tomorrow.

2

      Squandered so much:

but most of all
      those long silences together,
sometimes at noon over lunch, sometimes
      very late at night
after a long day working, those
      we squandered most beautifully of all.

3

      One bird, then another

begins to sing
      outside the store
where you try on dresses.
      The black is beautiful,
but so, too, is the blue.

EXAMPLES

The pale green walls of the little room

we've been given to use.
     Or another example:
the calm way a siren sounds
     after six inches of snow.
Winter light, for sure,
     as the sound of your foot on the stair
grows fainter.

NOT TAKING IT PERSONALLY

1 (Thesis)

We go to the same café

as the twelve-step coffee drinkers.
    A new one today: young, shaky,
purple hair. Already, she smiles well.
    The hair will go soon,
smudged look in her eyes
      slowly drain away.
I've seen it all before:
    what happens, mother,
when they do finally stop.

2 (Antithesis)

In the room where the friends meet,

the thirteen-year-old boy sprawls.
    While the grown-ups talk,
he eats three Reese's Peanut Butter Cups
    in search of just the right amount
of sweetness. Only then,
    does he let himself fall asleep
as we go on worrying aloud
    about the world.
We stare at him as we speak,
    as those who are lonely
will stare into a fire late at night
    seeing there the world as we wish it were.

3 (Synthesis)

Each song on the CD

more sad than the one before.
I need to remember
I'm not the first, won't be the last.

MY FAME

Don't think I didn't want it.

But moonlight distracted me. Even dust
     in sunlight in summer
distracted. Both
     were my friends, knew me
for who I was,
     forgave me everything.

BLIZZARD

DAY 1

As snow begins to fall,

a cement mixer slowly turns, so patiently,
     across the street under bare January branches.
How I wish I were the man I'm not.

DAY 2

Snow blocks the bridge.

No one can cross.
     How sad life is,
how calm.

DAY 3

My beard grows white.

I could say like waves or like snow;
     but really,
white like an old man's beard.

HER BITTERNESS MAKES SENSE—

old, blind, affronted—but still
     I would hope for her
this short April dusk,
     as yet unspoken for.

TRUE ENOUGH,

I have forgotten many things.
But I do remember
        the bank of clover along the freeway
we were passing thirty years ago
        when someone I loved made clear to me
it was over.

PIGEONS IN A BLACK SKY,

flying straight into the rain
      on white wings, moving far away
from the very idea of day and night
      into pure storm, never once
looking back: the way they say
      the dying don't,
once it is clear
      how this world
is such a small beginning.

ON THE DAY AFTER

The old woman who lives across the street

runs her vacuum
        on the day after Christmas,
cleaning up after the silence
        of the day before.
Two small geraniums in the window
        lean into one another
like people whispering at a funeral:
        signs of life.

GRADUALLY, THAT HALF-SMILE

my father so often wore as he got older
    takes me on as a project.

AFTER LIFE

1

In her last days

my aunt marveled at how kind everyone was.
        All they wanted of her
was that she swallow her pills.
        They even broke them in half.
Still, she couldn't do it.
        She had just enough energy left
to be moved by kindness; not a bit more.

2

It's not anything

you can take with you
        into the next world,
this dawn.

3

Who would have thought,

sunlight, tugboat's
        thick black smoke, this slow river,
who would have thought
        nothing ends?

4

I decide not to bother

putting a new battery in the clock:
        7 A.M. for good now, new light in the trees
and a small wind that will go on forever.

MY SWALLOWS AGAIN

(Spoleto)

Early morning: cuckoos and swallows crying out as if it's the first time ever.

The sound of hammers.

The way sunlight looks on the Scotch broom growing on the side of the hill across the valley from our window: how even after all these years I keep thinking I'll find the right words to say it all.

I don't sleep much, but this tiredness helps me see the man by the side of the road, holding a heavy bag of groceries and waiting for the bus while he leans against a light pole, eyes closed.

Staring at the cloudy sky, I try to act as if this sadness is just what I need.

It was only this one time we lived, you in your black T-shirt, standing next to an olive tree, sun shining down, and me frowning a little so I could see you all the more clearly.

Isn't there some way to finish this life sitting at an open window on a rainy day listening to birds call out?

Inside of life, and inside of death, swallows keep flying.

A small deer runs across my path and suddenly I am no longer lonely.

My swallows again. And yet, I couldn't stop myself thinking about what would happen should you go first.

Olive trees about the size of people; so quiet near dusk, their silver leaves. And their way of not minding my troubled thoughts.

If my parents had graves, it's on a warm cloudy day like this I would go to visit them.

Stupid teenage boys grin their stupid grins and honk their horn at you while you stand motionless under your dark cloth. Thank God I was never sixteen.

Saw that old man again today, the one who looks down at each step he takes, as if needing to convince himself that there is somewhere else he needs to go.

Rain every day for two weeks, wet olive trees, wet poppies, you under an umbrella, laughing.

First they tear up the old sidewalk, then put in the new one. I hope they understand how short life is.

The swallows are leaving; maybe going away is a thing I too can do with a little flourish and swoop at the end.

The old man in suit and tie sits on the park bench, leans forward in his elegant way so he won't miss a word of what the girl with the tattoo is trying to explain to him. Even at this distance I can see he doesn't have a clue, his happiness as complete as his confusion.

A woman feeds her sister's cat each morning while the sister is gone. *Amore, amore,* she calls and the cat comes. I sit in the shadows, my death nearby, neither of us minding the presence of the other.

My friend's hands tremble from his illness as he makes the ice cream using fresh melon, then spots it with a touch of some dark liqueur.

It may be that dying is a little like leaving Spoleto: all this confusion and worry about catching a train that is only going to Perugia.

Seagulls crying out in the piazza. What are they doing here so far from the sea?

How can you not love a country where the meter maids wear high heels?

On the other side of the mountain, where I cannot see, I'm sure another old man must sit, just as I do now, like this on a couch in his bathrobe, lonely and happy.

TWENTY QUESTIONS:
NEW POEMS

(2014)

TWENTY QUESTIONS

Did I forget to look at the sky this morning
when I first woke up? Did I miss the willow tree?
The white gravel road that goes up from the cemetery,
but to where? And the abandoned house on the hill, did it get
even a moment? Did I notice the small clouds so slowly
moving away? And did I think of the right hand
of God? What if it is a slow cloud descending
on earth as rain? As snow? As shade? Don't you think
I should move on to the mop? How it just sits there, too often
unused? And the stolen rose on its stem?
Why would I write a poem without one?
Wouldn't it be wrong not to mention joy? Sadness,
its sleepy-eyed twin? If I'd caught the boat
to Mykonos that time when I was nineteen
would the moon have risen out of the sea
and shone on my life so clearly
I would have loved it
just as it was? Is the boat
still in the harbor, pointing
in the direction of the open sea? Am I
still nineteen? Going in or going out,
can I let the tide make of me
what it must? Did I already ask that?

IN MY DREAM

I called out for a dog: two came.
      One was old and black, very slow

to mind. One was young and golden,
      she came in a blaze of delight.

I was given two dogs.
      They both stayed by my side.

LAST SUNDAY AFTERNOON

I lay on the bed like a dead man.
You could call it rest, but really:
I would never move again.

When I did get up, the spring light
had already gone dark. My friend came to me.
Together we walked toward dinner.

Tulips and daffodils.
Small scattered kingdoms of violets.
Take a left, then a right. Then walk and walk.

I asked my friend, whose life now
is difficult beyond my understanding,
"What are you feeling?"

"That's not the point," she said,
a little anger in her voice.
We were walking past the corner

where I had lived as a young man,
the same corner
where I had denied love.

Now Somalis live there, purple
robes and white caps
the color of doves in sunlight.

She was speaking of ancient Greek sculpture.
How she prefers them headless, since then
she can imagine, without the restraint

of the actual, tenderness in the eyes
and around the edges
of their down-turned mouths.

BE CAREFUL,

or your fears will chase off the red-winged blackbirds
        who live in the tall grasses by the path
near the fake dairy.
        You will be so alone.

KEEP IT

I had borrowed my friend's vest.
For two months, wore it daily.
It kept me warm. And reminded me of him

when I was lonely. He had gone somewhere south,
but I had stayed in the cold.
When he returned, I scrubbed out the spots

and took it back to him. "Did you like it?"
he asked, his hand trembling,
for my friend is ill.

"Loved it," I said. "Keep it," he said.
We were standing in the dark,
but still I could see that he was smiling.

The stars shone.
I put it on,
my vest.

ARS POETICA

The poets of certitude use words I'd like to use:
magnificence,
libation,
shining.

Meanwhile, at 7 A.M., eleven floors below, the man at the flower store
wears a black coat against the chill. Out go the pots on the sidewalk:
roses, probably; certainly daffodils,
as it is spring.
Every morning, the same task: I watch him closely.
Not once does he look up.
Beauty,
the ordinary kind, noted
as an afterthought,
if at all.

AT THE MET

The Buddha is smiling
and at the same time casts down his eyes,
    as Buddha does so like to do,
as if a little afraid
    to look at us.
Perhaps he has seen enough
    of this world.
Someone enters
    from another gallery and says
to a friend coming up behind him,
    "Nothing here."

INSOMNIA

3 A.M. and a full moon.
Happiness is not his specialty: this much
can't be argued. He remembers the night he met her,
twenty-five years ago. She sat on the couch.
That black hair; those eyes. Later,
they talked for hours in someone else's kitchen.

In the moonlight, he sees the branches of the tree,
grown large during those twenty-five years.
Sometimes she's bossy. Often he's just impossible.

Inch by inch, the moon sets behind the alley
where each morning they walk the dog,
silken ears up, outrageous tail spread wide,
fanning the air for all the world to see
what an honor it is, leading the way home
on this magnificent day.

I KEPT HOPING THERE MIGHT BE AN EASIER WAY,

even after Berryman
    and how his hand shook
when he spoke with us, his students,
    of those he loved:
Saint Augustine, Anne Frank, an old Zen master,
    so it was said,
beyond distinguishing between words
    like *life* and *death.*
Berryman's voice quavered
    when he whispered to the class, intimately,
as if to a lover in bed,
    "Here are the truest words Christ ever spoke,
My God, my God,
    why have you forsaken me?"

MY SENTENCE: TODAY I DO KNOW IT

Maybe because it's the first day of the New Year,
    today I know that sitting at a window

        and looking out at a gray sky, snow falling

so finely, like mist, like fog, today I know
    that sitting and waiting for a poem,

        sitting unsuccessfully

while watching the black smokestack across the river,
    tall and solitary and reminding me

        of the dignity hiding

within loneliness,
    today I know that waiting,

        then happening

to look up at just the moment
    when the streetlights go off

        at 8:23 A.M.

(for the day truly is dark, dark almost
    beyond endurance),

        today I know as I pause,

consider the stone arches of the old bridge-
    striations of mist, and uncertain light, the curtain

        of fog, transparent, which blurs the world finally

into blue uncertainty—today I know
    that to sit like this and to fail

        to write the poem

is precisely the fate—
    the exact level of insurmountable difficulty—

        which I have been given in order to grasp

what I can of the world as it actually is,
    only *grasp* is the wrong verb entirely, rather,

        to be submerged in, bathed in, as the baby

is bathed, baptized, in those old paintings,
    the holy crying out, the baby trying to swim away,

        but he can't escape,

that's not what happens, you don't reach
    dry land,

        you stay like this, just like this,

whichever direction you look
    the blowing snow, the mist and fog, and today

        I do know this much: the hell

of longing for life to be what it's not must now come
    to an end for me, on this the beginning

        of the newest year yet lived by anyone, ever, on earth.

29 STILLNESSES

Prayer is a giving thanks for the stillness it interrupts.

Outside, two voices say it back and forth, the only word stillness has ever bothered to learn: "Good-bye," "Good-bye."

Writing poems about stillness is like crying fire in an empty theater.

Don't make the mistake of calling out to stillness, *friend*. Friends need us. Stillness doesn't need us.

Even stillness will turn against you if you try to use it to ask directions.

Each time stillness leaves me, I feel betrayed as if for the first time.

Every morning at dawn the crooked tree comes back from the darkness, like an old retired professor. The professor emeritus of stillness, refusing to give up even on his slowest student.

Death needs us to love stillness, if we are to know how to give back our lives when the time comes.

Remember how much like a spy you felt the very first time you saw someone you loved lost inside her own stillness?

It was summer: nearby us, mountains rose up behind the lawn chair where she sat. She sat quietly, as if quiet were the most natural thing in the world. Whoever sees their mother's stillness, even once, will never forget.

My father liked to get up early and sit at his desk, looking out the window. Like me, he pretended, even to himself, that in stillness he was working.

Stillness loves that dream where you find the wooden box with no handles: you can't be expected to lift what can't be held.

Sometimes at night moonlight can show me where I mislaid my stillness.

It's true: I only know stillness when the world around me is still. The dog's toenails click on the wooden floor as she runs in her sleep.

Do you think stillness is always easy? Think of the moment she gets into bed for the first time alone, the widow.

Loneliness is like stillness, except for the fear inside it.

All stillness needs from me is to remember I will die.

Wonderful as it is, stillness cannot warm these cold feet.

Failure: no more interesting than success, but its one virtue is that it makes room for stillness.

Mary is stillness in those paintings. What is fear to her now that she knows love and the end of love are one and the same?

Stillness in the cathedral after the funeral: an old man walks from pew to pew, collecting the abandoned programs.

Stillness: the art of making nothing out of nothing.

The pink house across the street will always be too pink. Even at dawn, even under the full moon. Not even stillness can save the pink house from itself.

Today I wake up late. Already it has begun to grow light and stillness has packed its bags to begin the long trip back to the lilac bush inside which, when I was nine, I would hide for hours at a time.

This morning is stillness: even the crow forgets to cry out at the injustice of it all.

When I die, the stillness inside me, condemned to serve out its time behind the thick bars of language, will at last be pardoned.

Every stillness has a story behind it, an excuse for why it is so late in arriving.

Moonlight falls on old snow as stillness falls on ancient griefs.

Stillness: would I have traded it in for a happy life?

(2000–2013)

DARK EYE

(after a poem by Tarjei Vesaas)

A dark eye rests on us.
Wherever we are, the dark eye follows

in the stillness of the park. And by the river

where the water shone on the day he died, the brother of our friend.
From inside the wet grasses,

the dark eye shining. See the broken spokes of the shopping cart?

Someone has wheeled it to the river, has left it there.
And the dark eye is with us as we walk past.

Johnny

was the name of the brother. Johnny who lived by the ocean.
Who loved the waves. Who sat on a little porch, listening to
the waves.

In his sickness, he listened.

When night comes,
sometimes we are afraid. Sometimes when the wind stirs.

But the dark eye protects us. Yes, even when I was in prison.

Even when the bomb in the airport went off and those twelve people died,
a floor beneath me.

Even after I was taken against my will.

Dark eye, with a tear for my mother, her head tipped into her drink, face
gone slack.
People sometimes turn away. Very suddenly people will turn around

because they fear the dark eye.

The dark eye is near. Very near.
    When the blackest part of the night comes,

that's when the eye stirs just enough to help us see.

I DRANK THREE GLASSES OF MONTEFALCO RED,

then walked to the aqueduct in the mist-
      wanting-to-be-rain. To myself I chanted,
in Italian, the future of *to want*. I was laughing
      the whole time, but my face was wet,
as though with tears.

VARIATION ON A POEM BY DU FU

It aches, this life. When I quit trying
to say it is otherwise, I feel relieved.
So many people I love are in such pain.
When grief comes, it comes

and comes. The truth, you say?
I don't bother to get dressed some days.
Yesterday, I saw that apple tree
in the old Jewish cemetery.

Blossoms fell as a man walked by,
whistling. Stones gleamed in sunlight.
A wrought-iron fence guarded the dead,
kept out the living. There are no words for it,

how sunlight shines on the fence
that separates the living from the dead.

YESTERDAY

He was as calm as he always is,
my older friend whose diagnosis
is sooner rather than later.
Together we sat at his window,
looking out at the Mississippi
and the barely visible cut
of the new moon in the darkening sky.
"How's the poetry business?"
he asked, with that little smile of his.
"Not so good," I said, then amended it,
"Good enough," and gave him
my own little smile in return.

The sea gulls at the river were strangely quiet,
and the bare branches of the cottonwoods stood still
inside their abundant patience. It was that time
when the streetlights come on over the bridge.
My fearful heart. These few poems
I've tried to make. It was that time
when an old man looks
toward the door, meaning
by the slight tilt of his head,
not bothering to speak:
go now.

LATE SUMMER SLOWLY INSISTING

1

I say, "I could eat coronetti all day long."

A blind man, unshaven, hangs on to his bored son's arm.

The slow insistent tidal waves of morning's crickets
        and the uncut meadow's long sun-darkened grasses.

I won't ever find it, the peace I always sought.

Amazing how I never understood before:
        how mist on the river works,
        complaining doesn't.

The neon cross above Monteluco, sunlit and skeletal by day:
        for twenty-seven years now
        it's been trying to teach us—
        two shy monolinguals—
        how to pronounce *death,*
        then a little too quickly afterward,
        resurrection.

I pick up a newspaper, but put it down fast.

2

I couldn't care less about them yesterday,
        and now this morning,
        as we talk of your shoes that are too tight,
        for some reason, I do.

Night arrives still so late in August, aqueduct
    rising out of the darkness.
    I must not forget to say that young ones
    sometimes come to stand on its edge,
    hold hands, then jump to their deaths.

A stooped man on a park bench moves a little to the right
    so that his dog panting in the sun can lie in shadow,
    a creature who, like all of us, has suffered
    more than his share, like all of us has known joy unexpected
    as a sudden shadow on a day almost too hot to bear.

A woman half my age laughs at my silly joke: she seems to really mean it.

3

White stars, on a moonless night sting like first snow
    when I walk past the aqueduct at 1 A.M.

No more father and mother,
    son or daughter.

Today's words are *sadness, fear, wind*. Today's other word is *patience*.

And *smokestacks* as they hold up the horizon inside this darkness.

Not a peep out of the cuckoo who hides in the neighborhood cypress.

These Fra Filippo Lippi saints look on the wrinkled postcard
    I carry everywhere I go. Bald-headed men like me.
    There is worry in the eyes, and, yes, fear, too.
    Lippi fills those four anxious faces with light.
    They cast a faint glow, like streetlights on a rainy night,
    showing us where to turn next.

4

"Why do I find it so hard to be kind?" the man asked me, tears in his eyes:
but he was asking the wrong person.

The way there are bales of hay stacked in the far meadow,
as yet unspoken for, still bound to this earth.

That angel on top of the church near dusk:
ugly as sin, but I will admit

to walk under its frowning brow

is more than a little part of this darkness, late,
awkward brooding wings, all of it

earmarked as ours as if for some reason we had been told,

28 years ago: *Go there. Never ever leave,
except to return.* And I must not forget

the pen you stole for me from Bar Canasta.

Tulips bloomed in that shadowy courtyard
and a girl skipped rope, while a man in a wheelchair sighed

so deeply it seemed all sadness had a way

of breathing in, before simply growing bored,
then disappearing once and for all. How often that pen

has tried to explain how it is that we finished up like this,
sitting on a bench under an almond tree

in late summer in last light

as bells begin ringing again from that ungainly church,
for no reason except that another day

has somehow managed to make it all the way

to 7:02 P.M. A man in sandals with braids
down to his belt cries out, "Bella, Bella!"

into his little phone as he looks out toward the Apennines,

barely visible, skittering away uncertainly
in this day's last light tinted the blued orange

Fra Filippo used for Mary's sky as she lies there dying

in the Duomo down the hill. It's fading quickly,
this August dusk, demanding the man pocket

his phone, and lean forward, further and further, all the way

into evening. The wiry mutt at his side pushes against him, alert,
ears cocked, such a puzzled look on its face,

as if it sees something amazing.

Exactly what it is
who can possibly begin to say, but you and I?

UNDERGROUND

1

    A little shaky,

I sit in the subway car, watching a woman read.
      Slowing my breath to match hers,
we travel together under the earth.

2

    A man in a business suit, my age,

gray hair, working his Blackberry—
      hunched over, newspaper
balanced on one knee, head bowed as if in prayer:
      brother, should we cry? Laugh?

3

    A woman sleeps next to me. What luck

to see loneliness
      given rest.

4

    "It's coming so fast,"

says an old woman across from me,
      speaking to no one in particular:

she nods her head in agreement with herself
      and strictly speaking
who can argue with her?

MEANWHILE,

     my old friend, her face taken over
by grief, talks
     with such sweetness to a stray cat:
I rest my case.

LIFE: A DISAPPEARANCE

1

Weren't the four black smokestacks a part of it?
And the rainy wind blowing birds back and forth?
And the lights
coming on toward nightfall as beautiful
as beautiful could be?
Weren't the October leaves?
Wasn't there first the slow touching
and then the urgent? But, oh, those leaves—
to answer your question
about why I've spent my life
writing poetry—
their strange smell of
rot and spice,
it takes a whole lifetime, after all,
to acquire the nose for it.

2

And the rainy wind blowing birds back and forth?
And the lights
as beautiful could be?
Wasn't there first the slow touching
to answer your question
writing poetry—
it takes a whole lifetime, after all,

3

as beautiful could be?
Wasn't there first the slow touching
rot and spice,
to answer your question

4

Weren't the October leaves?
coming on toward nightfall as beautiful
writing poetry—

5

it takes a whole lifetime, after all,

NOTES

A few early poems have been revised from their published versions.

Writing with Tagore: Homages and Variations

The Indian writer Rabindranath Tagore's book *Gitanjali* was praised by W. B. Yeats and Ezra Pound among many others, and largely due to this book, Tagore received the Nobel Prize in Literature in 1913. The book was translated into English by Tagore himself and remains in print to this day all over the world.

For years I had wanted to somehow retranslate *Gitanjali,* even though the author himself did the original translation: his English felt dated and awkward to my ear. Then I realized I didn't want to translate the book, but rather do a book of my own poems that were homages and variations on Tagore's work, that borrowed images, phrases, tones, ideas from his poems, but borrowed them as a sail borrows wind before moving in a direction of its own.

Twenty Questions: New Poems

"Last Sunday Afternoon" is in memory of Sage Cowles.
"Keep It" is for Martin Stubenrauch.
"Ars Poetica" is for John Pankow, Elenore Pankow, and Kristine Sutherland.
"Dark Eye" is for Joyce Kobayashi.
"Yesterday" is in memory of John Cowles.
"Late Summer Slowly Insisting" is for Mariella Badiali.

ACKNOWLEDGMENTS

I want to acknowledge and thank my many friends in poetry and fellow writers who have made so much difference to me as a writer these last fifty years:

Peggy Berg, Robert Bly, Jill Breckenridge, Michael Dennis Browne, Don Brunnquell, Emilie Buchwald, Marisha Chamberlain, Carol Conroy, Patricia Francisco, Margot Kriel Galt, David Goldes, Joseph Goldes, Nor Hall, Patricia Hampl, Phebe Hanson, Margaret Hasse, Annie Hayes, Jane Hilberry, Nelson Hinds, Jane Hirshfield, Tony Hoagland, Lewis Hyde, Joel Janowitz, Deborah Keenan, Sandy Kinnee, Patricia Kirkpatrick, Joyce Kobayashi, Jim Krusoe, Julie Landsman, Jonathan Lee, Miriam Levine, Gretchen Marquette, David Mason, Gail Mazur, Bill Mohr, Carol Moldaw, Sheryl Mousley, David Mura, Alice Quinn, Mary Rockcastle, Wendy Salinger, Bart Schneider, Arthur Sze, Katrina Vandenberg, Carol Venezia, Michael Venezia, and Jay White.

I also want to thank my students who move me and make me laugh and trust me with their poems.

Three teachers made a huge difference: John Berryman, Toni McNaron, and George Starbuck.

And two teachers outside the classroom: Meridel LeSueur and Tom McGrath.

The Press at the Colorado College for their beautiful edition of the Tagore poems and to Accordion Productions for another beautiful book, *What It's Like Here.*

Thanks to those blessed souls who read poetry because life without it feels impossible.

And to Graywolf Press: Fiona McCrae, Jeff Shotts, and Marisa Atkinson.

JoAnn Verburg's photographs have appeared on the covers of six of my books. It's been a wonderful thing for me that they have accompanied my work over the years as it has made its way into the world.

———

I also acknowledge with much gratitude a fellowship from the John Simon Guggenheim Foundation that helped significantly in the work of putting together this book.

———

I'd like to acknowledge the following publications for publishing new poems:

The Academy of American Poets on its Poem-A-Day website
Poetry City, USA (Vol. 4)
Sleet
32 Poems

JIM MOORE is the author of eight previous books of poetry, one in collaboration with Deborah Keenan. His work has appeared in the *American Poetry Review*, the *Antioch Review*, *Harper's*, the *Kenyon Review*, the *Nation*, the *New Yorker*, the *Paris Review*, *Sleet*, *Water~Stone Review*, and many other magazines, as well as in two editions of the *Pushcart Prize Anthology*. The poem "For You" was also reprinted in *The Pushcart Book of Poetry*. An excerpt of his poem "Love in the Ruins" appeared in New York subways and buses as part of the Poetry Society of America's Poetry in Motion initiative. He is the recipient of fellowships from the Bush Foundation, the Jerome Foundation, the McKnight Foundation, the Minnesota State Arts Board, and most recently the Guggenheim Foundation. Moore has taught in various universities and colleges, most recently in the MFA program at Hamline Univesity in Saint Paul, Minnesota, and the Colorado College in Colorado Springs, Colorado. He and his wife, the photographer JoAnn Verburg, live in Minneapolis and in Spoleto, Italy.

The text of *Underground* is set in Adobe Caslon Pro. Book design by Rachel Holscher. Composition by BookMobile Design and Publishing Services, Minneapolis, Minnesota. Manufactured by Versa Press on acid-free, 30 percent postconsumer wastepaper.